She's Ready at 18… He's Ready at 38!

She's Ready at 18...

He's Ready at 38!

Calvin Brown

Pearly Gates Publishing, LLC, Houston, Texas (USA)

She's Ready at 18… He's Ready at 38!

She's Ready at 18… He's Ready at 38!

Copyright © 2021
Calvin Brown

All Rights Reserved.
No portion of this publication may be reproduced, stored in an electronic system, or transmitted in any form or by any means (electronic, mechanical, photocopy, recording, or otherwise) without written permission from the author or publisher. Brief quotations may be used in literary reviews.

Print ISBN 13: 978-1-948853-30-9
Digital IBSN 13: 978-1-948853-31-6
Library of Congress Control Number: 2021911175

This is a work of fiction. Names, characters, businesses, events, and incidents are the products of the author's imagination. Any resemblance to actual persons, living or dead, or actual events is purely coincidental.

Scripture references are taken from the King James Version (KJV) of the Holy Bible and used with permission via Zondervan. Public Domain.

For information and bulk ordering, contact:
Pearly Gates Publishing, LLC
Angela Edwards, CEO
P.O. Box 62287
Houston, TX 77205
BestSeller@PearlyGatesPublishing.com

Calvin Brown

Dedication

This novel is dedicated to **ALL** marriages.

Acknowledgments

Thank you, **Almighty Father, Jesus Christ, and the Holy Spirit,** for allowing this novel to be released at the appointed time.

Secondly, I thank my awesome, amazing, beautiful, loving, and Heaven-sent wife, **Kenya Brown,** who has provided me the unconditional support that was very beneficial to me as I completed this book.

Lastly, I thank **everyone** who provided continued encouragement, moral support, and assisted in completing this work.

Calvin Brown

Introduction

Being married is more than just being in a relationship. Marriage is a major commitment with many internal obligations. Some refer to it as:

- ➤ Project management
- ➤ A game of chess or checkers
- ➤ An open book
- ➤ A rollercoaster
- ➤ Paradise
- ➤ A box of chocolates
- ➤ Always predictable
- ➤ A dream…or nightmare
- ➤ One of their best decisions

Other explanations include those who are afraid to commit because they have heard countless horror stories about the experience. Conversely, others say marriage helped save their lives and wouldn't want to live without it. Essentially, it is what you make it to be.

Matrimony is a collaborative effort to maintain love, peace, trust, unity, strength, progress, romance, and so much more. When everything flows properly, marriage is like poetic teamwork. It is the quintessential love partnership — if you have a suitable mate who would also be your peace mate.

Marriage must be maintained better than a manicured lawn, as it has more than four seasons and must always be watered with love. There are numerous books, movies, and songs about it, but none have yet to define the depths of the commitment thoroughly. If it seems like a mystery, let love provide the solution.

On the list of factors on maintaining a healthy marriage is this: Both parties must address their expectations and dynamics before taking their vows. There are many to be discussed, with one of the most important being the age factor—if there is one. Age can be an issue if the intricacies of the age difference in the marriage are not adequately highlighted and thoroughly discussed before marriage.

In some instances, the youngest one in the marriage is still maturing, while the oldest might be stuck in their ways. Then, there are times when the youngest one is as mature as the oldest. There are also instances when the age difference is tolerated for selfish reasons, not because it is true love. No matter the circumstance, the man and woman in the marriage must deal with one another and not worry about who is judging them—although that is often inevitable. In some cultures, the age difference would not be an issue. However, in America and Europe, significant age differences are not considered "normal." As a result, it would not be surprising if the oldest of the two was judged more harshly than their younger counterpart.

People will always have something to say, especially the parents of a young lady. Most parents have already dreamt of a fairytale future for their baby girl, and virtually none of them included her with a man twice her age. In that case, they would likely view the older man as a "Sugar Daddy" who swept their daughter off her feet because he could provide for her much better than any young man her age. In some instances, the older man's intentions would be questioned as "having a fancy for the young ladies." Then, there is a rare matter where the young lady is as mature and built like a 40-year-old woman, which could have been the way she hooked that older man. Many other good and bad theories could be used to judge them, but they must live their lives focused on their marriage…and peace.

Regardless of the opinions of others, peace must remain the couple's goal. As long as deceit or immoral actions did not contribute to the union, they should be left alone to live their happy lives together.

Still, a May/December union can be a tough pill to swallow, especially if it happens to you. Think about it: What if a 38-year-old man came to your door and told you he wanted to marry your 18-year-old daughter who lives at home with you? What if he was a known womanizer 20 years ago? What do you imagine your initial reaction to his request would be? It is common for people to pass judgment on others, but it is a whole new ball game when it hits home.

Seriously, though, I must ask again: What do you imagine your initial reaction to his request would be? Take some time to explain the scenario to a few friends and see what they say. The reactions will likely vary, but you will find that if they are not prepped for the question, their first reaction would be outright negative—and THAT would be the genuine response. I encourage you to give it a try.

This book is intended to be a tool of inspiration to help build and strengthen marriages—no matter the age difference. As you turn from page to page, place yourself in the shoes of the characters and constantly ask yourself:

What would I do?

She's Ready at 18… He's Ready at 38!

Table of Contents

Dedication vi

Acknowledgments vii

Introduction viii

Who Is She? 1

Chapter One: Is She Ready? 2

Chapter Two: Friends 20

Chapter Three: Secrets 36

Chapter Four: The Truth Hurts 47

Chapter Five: First Fight 58

Chapter Six: Dealing With It 69

Chapter Seven: Wedding Week 77

    Bachelor and Bachelorette Parties 78

    Wedding Day 84

Nuggets for the Readers 88

    For the Singles 88

    For the Married: Praying and Fasting 89

Wisdom Nuggets 91

Relationship Quotes 96

Are You Thinking About Marriage? 99

Three Phases of Life 100

Due Diligence Assistance 103

Hurdles or Walls 107

Skin Deep 112

Mates 113

Biblical Principles of Marriage 114

    The Husband 114

The Wife 118
The Union 121
Your Lawn (Relationship) 125
About the Author 126

She's Ready at 18… He's Ready at 38!

Who Is She?

She is dressed in a wedding gown.

She is sitting in a chair in a room alone with her head down, praying.

She is finished praying and decides to join her bridesmaids.

She is now standing.

She is heading to exit the room just as someone knocks on the door and reminds her the wedding is about to start.

She is smiling as she opens the door…

Chapter One: Is She Ready?

It's Friday night, and four friends—one married—meet at the local lounge to enjoy their monthly outing. They arrive in the parking garage of the lounge called "Top Shelf" at around the same time. Top Shelf is a high-end lounge that only serves wine. While standing outside of their cars, Olivia asks, "What if your 18-year-old daughter was seriously interested in a 38-year-old man?" Everyone gave their honest opinion, with all of them basically not approving of such an arrangement. "I should have Spartan-kicked and shot him! What does a grown man want with my baby?" Olivia states with exasperation before telling her story.

****

"One early evening, I received a call from Lizzie [her daughter] telling me she would be home in ten minutes. She went on to say she wanted me to meet her boyfriend and that she believed he wanted to propose to her. I told her okay and then told Michael [Lizzie's father]. You know he was not excited one bit but agreed to be nice about the situation.

About ten minutes later, after hanging up from Lizzie, someone rang our doorbell. I was closest to the door since I was downstairs cooking at the time, so I answered it. When I opened the door, Ricky was standing on our porch. You remember handsome Ricky Randolph, right? The one we went to high school with? I immediately flashed back to when he and I kissed in school. We had just started a relationship, but he dumped me for one of the more "popular" girls. In his last two years of high school, that boy had at least five different girlfriends. Eventually, I got over him, yet there he stood on my doorstep. I'm married and all, but he still looked like the same edible arrangement from back in the day! I had to catch myself, y'all! Anyway....

He was obviously startled, too, when he saw me. I asked him if he was lost, selling insurance now, or up to some crazy network marketing scheme since he was always into some type of business. Before he could answer, Lizzie stepped up from behind him, smiling and excited. I asked her why she was smiling from ear to ear, and that's when she told me: RICKY is her boyfriend!

I gave Ricky the look of next-level anger, to say it mildly, spoke some choice words to him, and then went to retrieve my husband's rifle. While I was walking away, I heard Lizzie tell him to run because she already knew the deal. By the time I returned to the porch, he was hightailing out of the driveway. He didn't get away scot-free, though. I shot out his back window. Michael came running downstairs, snatched the rifle from me, and told Lizzie and me to get inside.

Within five minutes, there were about four sheriff's cars in front of our house. Apparently, the neighbors called 911. Being that Michael is the County Sheriff, he got into his own sheriff's car, and they all followed after Ricky. A few miles away from our house, a sheriff's deputy already had Ricky standing outside his car in handcuffs. I had to laugh when I heard he was pulled over for excessive speeding. At the time he was pulled over, the deputy heard the dispatch informing all cars about shots being fired on the County Sheriff's property, that the man was driving a red, expensive luxury car, and he had fled the residence.

Michael said that when he arrived on the scene, he told the deputy he needed to speak to Ricky alone, so the deputy walked Ricky to my husband's car and set him inside. Just as Ricky was being put in the car, more deputies arrived, which scared the mess out of him because one of his friends had forewarned him about Michael. They told him the reason crime is virtually nonexistent in the county was that Lizzie's father is relentless when it comes to keeping order, to the point that criminals actually fear him. Keep in mind Michael and his deputies are all Caucasians and that Ricky is African American. Ricky didn't know, but the deputies thought he had assaulted Lizzie.

My husband said he told Ricky he was disgusted with him but that since our daughter was not a minor, there was nothing he could do. Still, he promised Ricky that if he catches him in our county again, it would be a bad experience for him. Ricky knew not to say anything because he was severely outnumbered. Plus, he was blocked on all sides by the deputies' cars. Michael said Ricky peed his pants when he looked out of his window and saw all those officers staring at him with rage in their eyes. Michael said Ricky likely misheard a comment made about Lizzie being assaulted by him, which probably convinced him the deputies were ready to kill him on the spot. After my husband saw that Ricky peed his pants, he reached back and removed the handcuffs, but Ricky remained in place and speechless because he really thought his life was going to end right then and there.

When Michael told Ricky the deputies really believed he assaulted Lizzie, Ricky begged my husband to please tell them the truth because he would never do anything to hurt our daughter. My husband grabbed the microphone in his car and told the deputies Lizzies wasn't assaulted and that it was just a misunderstanding. He then turned back to Ricky and once again promised him that if he is caught in our county again, it would not be pretty, to which Ricky promised and timidly asked Michael if he was free to leave. Michael got out, opened his rear door, and gestured for Ricky to exit. Ricky ran to his car and, as he drove off, the deputies started clinching their fists because they knew he was looking at them in his rearview mirror. You see, although all the deputies were Caucasian, half of them are in interracial marriages like Michael and me.

Michael eventually made it back home and confronted Lizzie. At the time, she and I were sitting in the living room waiting for him. As soon as he sat down, Lizzie told us about Ricky. She said that she likes him for many things but mostly because he believes in her, he has not tried to have sex with her, he is obviously mature, she feels safe with him, he's a great listener, he has his own home and his finances are in order, he doesn't pressure her, he's not controlling, he goes to church, and the list goes on. When I asked her how she met him, she said they met at the bookstore when he had a book signing event. She went on to say that he only came to the house after she pressured him to do so. Rather defiantly, she told us she would not stop seeing him and that if he wanted to marry her, there is nothing we could do about it because she is of age. At that, Michael stood and walked upstairs without saying another word. As for me, I just sat there in silence because I was still in shock."

When Olivia stopped talking, all her friends stared at her in shocked silence because they didn't know what to say. Out of nowhere, she busted out in uncontrollable laughter. After she calmed a bit, Sarah told her to explain the laughter after telling such a weird story.

"I'm laughing because Ricky peed his pants! Can you imagine? Remember: Ricky used to always act like he was the toughest guy in the city—and for a time, I believed he was. But to know that he peed his pants proved that he was all hype. Plus, I laugh to help me not dwell on the situation, but it's hard because every single time I look at my daughter, I see her with him." That explanation did nothing to break the ice, so Olivia told them, "I need your help, ladies, to get through this situation. Ladies' night at the lounge is an excellent way to start!"

****

The friends were standing in the parking garage next to Sarah's car when Sarah told everyone to grab hands so that they could say a quick prayer for them like she always does. It might have seemed weird to anyone else for them to pray before going into a lounge, but that didn't stop Sarah. During the prayer, she mentioned Olivia's situation, too. After praying, Sarah said, "I feel within my spirit that something special is going to happen tonight."

Shortly afterward, the ladies were joking around about who was the most desperate of the three single women in the group to get married. They then engaged in a bet to see who would be the first one to leave that night with a guy. Amid the friendly jesting back and forth, Tiffany said, "Chelsea has wanted a husband for so long that she is dehydrated for one!" Everyone laughed, except for Chelsea. She looked bewildered at first but eventually joined the others and started laughing.

Smiling, Chelsea replied, "I bet all of you $20.00 each that Sarah will be the first one to leave with a guy tonight." The other ladies agreed to the bet and laughed even harder because Sarah had been celibate for ten years and was known as a classy girl who is hard to get. Sarah looked at Chelsea, saluted her, and then started laughing, too.

****

That night at the lounge was "Wear Your Work Clothes Night." As the ladies were still hanging out in the parking garage, they noticed three nice cars enter. Five extremely attractive men of various races got out of the cars dressed in business suits. Tiffany and Chelsea did their classic cat calls, causing all the men to smile. "We'll see all of you fine jewels inside," one of the gentlemen said. Before making their way in, they remained in the parking garage for a bit longer, watching other professional-looking men walk into the lounge. They then noticed a younger gentleman in overalls who appeared to be a construction worker. All the women except Sarah grinned as he walked by.

"Why are you grinning at me like that?" the mystery man asked.

Tiffany replied, "You know this is a high-end place full of professionals. Aren't you a little too young to be out here with these grown folks?"

"I'm in my late 20s and obviously old enough to get in this lounge. And I am a professional looking to me other professionals like you. I'm really here just to power down and enjoy the night after a long workweek," he said.

All the ladies were at least ten years his senior, yet they were quieted by his voice and appearance as he approached them. He was tall and good-looking but not the best-dressed out of all the men who had already entered the lounge. As he got closer, the friends could see he wore designer overalls—something that could not be seen from a distance.

Sarah stepped forward and introduced herself. "Hi. I'm Sarah," she said while extending her hand for a handshake.

"Hi, Sarah. I'm Jason. Nice to meet you. Shall we?" he asked as he took her hand in his. They then walked hand-in-hand into the lounge, leaving Chelsea and the other ladies speechless! As Sarah and Jason walked past them, they looked at the couple in disbelief.

"I told y'all! I won the bet! Now, give me my money!" Chelsea said while cracking up. Tiffany casually reminded her it wasn't official until Sarah left the lounge with Jason.

****

As they entered the lounge, they noticed many well-dressed guys knew Jason. One of the waitresses escorted them to the VIP section where they always sat, with a "plus one" visitor joining them. Once seated, Jason ordered a round of drinks for the ladies and him. Men continuously walked by their table and smiled at them, but none stopped to engage in conversation out of some strange respect for Jason.

After everyone received their drink, Jason asked, "Is there an issue regarding my age?"

"No. Not really," Chelsea replied immediately. "If you are mature and have your stuff together, there's no problem." She then gave a few more prerequisites and high-fived Olivia and Tiffany. "Tell us more about you, Jason."

"Well, I've been trying to build my legacy while following in my father's footsteps. He owned many businesses, and I'd like to do the same." The ladies smiled broadly when he told them about his current businesses, stocks, day trading, investments, charities he supported, and that he was a "Preacher's Kid."

Tiffany gave Sarah a side-wink and said to Jason, "You are worth millions, young man."

"I don't feel rich. I'm still working for my dad." The friends were further amazed when he explained how everyone in the lounge knew him.

"Why aren't you drinking any wine? The Bible does not say you cannot drink it," Tiffany inquired.

"I have never had the desire. As well, the time may come when I have to talk to someone about overcoming an addiction to alcohol, and I do not want them to leverage my drinking against their addiction. I sometimes volunteer to counsel men about life and their daily struggles."

All while Jason spoke, Sarah was smiling because she believed she finally met the right one, even though he was younger than her. On the other hand, Chelsea was irritated because it seemed as if she missed out on a good man.

"May I ask you a question, Jason?" Olivia asked.

"Yes."

"What would you do if your 18-year-old daughter brought home a 38-year-old boyfriend?"

Jason appeared to think for just a moment before responding. "I would be pissed! My initial reaction would most likely be to hurt the man. However, because I am a devout Christian, I would simply tell the man in the calmest way possible to get off my property to keep myself from succumbing to the anger."

All the ladies smiled and were pleased with his response, especially Olivia, who shared with him an abbreviated version of the story about Lizzie and Ricky. They watched as Jason's smile turned to a frown.

Once Olivia finished with her story, he then shared one of his own. "Church leadership recently asked me to provide counseling to a couple with a huge age difference between them. I asked that they give the task to another leader in the church who is more senior than I because I believe the couple's counseling will lead to marital counseling. Since I have never been married, I am sure a leader with marital experience would be better equipped to assist that couple." The ladies couldn't help but be impressed. "Now, I am of the opinion that Ricky should have avoided coming to your house, knowing that he and Lizzie's age difference is a sensitive topic. He could have gotten hurt! Although there is no best way to approach the parents, if I were you, Olivia, I would have preferred he called first. Anything would have been better than him going to the house and knocking on your door!"

The group talked about the topic a little more before Olivia said she needed to move past it and simply enjoy the rest of their night.

As they chatted among themselves, Jason suddenly blurted out, "My main purpose for joining y'all tonight was to get to know Sarah since she was the only one who didn't prejudge me." Chelsea pinched herself under the table for letting him slip through her fingers. Jason then stood and motioned for the waitress to bring the ladies more wine. Once seated again, he said, "Let's talk about finances. What would each of you do if you received a million dollars?"

The ladies started speaking all at once, rather excitedly — except for Sarah, who was amazed at how easily Jason steered the attention completely away from the Lizzie and Ricky topic. When Jason noticed Sarah didn't answer the question, he looked her in the eyes and asked it again: "What would you do with a million dollars?"

Sarah paused, answered the question, and shortly after, the conversation turned much livelier as they laughed and laughed about one another's response. Time seemed to fly by that evening because they were having so much fun talking about the imaginary one million dollars. While the ladies continued discussing the question, Jason stood and asked, "Who wants to join me at the bar to help the waitress carry the drinks back to the table?" No one offered. They just gestured for him to go to the bar by himself. He then looked at Sarah and motioned for her to join him, but she shook her head no, choosing to remain at the table with her friends. Jason didn't know that none of them liked going to the bar because there was always some guy there with the same old tired lines trying to take one of them home for the night.

****

When Jason approached the bar, he saw some guys he knew, and they began to talk about sports. Shortly after, James walked up to the bar and was welcomed by an enthusiastic group of men. James was the local football star who left the city to enter the military since he did not receive scholarship offers from the top schools of his choice. "Hey, guys! It sure is good to be home. I finally retired and am ready to build a house here. It's time for me to settle down and truly rest," James announced. The men gave him high-fives and sentiments of appreciation for his service, while he thanked all of them for always supporting him.

Seeing the respect everyone gave James, Jason offered to buy him a drink. James gladly accepted and, along with the glass of wine, ordered himself a bottle. Although the two men didn't know each other, Jason appreciated the offer since he was often the one who bought rounds for everyone at the bar when he came home. While Jason continued talking to the bartender, James asked the guys to tell him about Jason. They all agreed and stated Jason was a cool guy who always tried to help everyone.

Shortly after, Jason approached the group of guys and formally introduced himself to James. The two men briefly embrace in a "nice-to-meet-you" manly greeting, after which Jason says to the men, "I have a question for y'all that the ladies asked me." Curious, the men fell silent and waited. "Okay. I see I have your attention." A quick burst of laughter flowed through the group. "What would you do if your 18-year-old daughter brought a 38-year-old man home and said he's her boyfriend?"

Almost all the men said they would most likely want to hurt the man. James, however, disagreed with them. He said, "If the young lady has done her research and the guy checks out, then I would have no choice but to respect my daughter's decision. Still, that would be a hard pill to swallow."

Jason gave them his response. "Yeah, I would be extremely upset with the guy but would stop short of resorting to violence against him."

"Why do you feel that way, Jason?" James asked.

"Well, I believe the man should be able to find someone his own age. Plus, if he's with a younger woman now, then what makes him not want someone younger once my daughter gets older?"

James smiled and told Jason, "You're overthinking it, man. You should simply respect your daughter's decision."

"Perhaps, but I don't have to worry about that anytime soon because I'm still young," Jason replied. The other guys nodded in agreement and laughed some more. As he walked away with the ladies' drinks in hand, James called out his name. Jason turned around, and James raised his glass of wine in salute with a smile on his face.

James watched as Jason approached the table with Sarah and the others. A frown washed over his face as he watched Jason sit next to Sarah after giving all the ladies their drinks. James seemed frozen in time as he continued to watch the two interact, with Sarah scooting closer to Jason and gazing into his eyes. James and Sarah were once a couple who used to sit in that same VIP section of the lounge many years ago. They have a daughter named Asia, but their marriage fell apart a few years after she was born.

As James stared at Jason and Sarah, Olivia took notice. She also remembered James' bad attitude, so she got up and walked over to greet him and soothe his mind. Olivia and Sarah were the closest of all the friends, and James respected her because she tried to keep Sarah and him together. "What's the deal with Jason?" James asked.

"He's a cool, young guy we just met tonight. I believe Sarah is just enjoying the night and not really that interested in Jason because he is too young for her." That brought James comfort because although they are not together, he still had feelings for his ex-girlfriend. "Would you like to join us at our table?" Olivia asked.

"No, thank you. Thanks for the offer. I'm home for good now just want to spend time with Asia. There will be other times we can all get together." As they stood there a while longer in silence, with James still keeping a watchful eye on the lovey-dovey couple across the room, he asked Olivia, "Why did you come over here?"

"It was no coincidence, James. My husband is right there."

James turned around and saw Michael staring at him. He stood, and the two men greeted one another. They were old friends who played football together. James also stopped a gang of guys in school from jumping Michael because of a misunderstanding. The two men reminisced for a few minutes before James felt it was time for him to get back to his own table. He hugged Michael and Olivia before walking away from the bar.

****

As James made his way through the bar, he saw an old high school football rival named Dave hanging out with some friends. When they see him coming their way, they stop talking and stand, prepared for whatever might happen between James and Dave. It was common knowledge that the two men got into a bad fight once during a football game, and they had not been friendly ever since. That particular game had many division-one college scouts in attendance, and when they saw James lose his cool on the field, he didn't receive a single scholarship offer. James blamed Dave for purposely setting him up to miss out on a golden opportunity to fulfill his dreams. After all, James was a senior at the time of the fight and had no other chance to redeem himself in front of the scouts. Dave, however, had already moved on from the incident and wanted to say something respectful to James that night at the lounge, but James didn't want to hear what he had to say. He purposely turned his back to Dave in an outright disrespectful manner and then walked away.

With a bottle of wine in hand, James walked up to his table where his girlfriend, Kelly, was seated and surrounded by some men standing and talking to her. Kelly was the CEO of an IT company who met James through a mutual friend. She was also an athlete at James' rival high school, but she was younger than him. James was noticeably upset about the guys talking to Kelly and then angrily introduced himself to them.

Kelly frowned at his behavior and calmly stated, "James, these are my cousins." Clearly embarrassed, James takes a seat next to Kelly.

"I like him!" one of the men said. "He was not afraid to step up!"

Another one said, "James, you have my approval to date Kelly," which brought a flood of laughter from the entire group.

When her cousins walked away, Kelly turned to James and said, "I am disappointed in how you acted."

"I'm sorry. I won't allow that to happen again."

"Who was the lady you were speaking to at the bar?" she asked. James told her about Olivia, the other women...and Dave. Being a non-confrontational person, Kelly said, "I think we should leave now before the wine gets the best of Sarah or Dave." James agreed.

Before leaving, however, the DJ gave James a shout-out. Upon hearing his name, the crowd starting chanting, "Hollywood James! Hollywood James! Hollywood James!" Kelly was amazed because many people took pictures of her and James as they were trying to leave. Although he did not go to college, everyone in the city still treated him like a celebrity.

Once outside, James asked Kelly if she could handle all the attention he gets. "I am used to it, James. When I go home, I get the same level of attention. Let me ask you: Can you handle me receiving all that attention?"

"I haven't seen that happen yet, but when the time comes, I believe I can handle it." No sooner than he said that, three guys walked past them. One of them recognized Kelly, screamed like a girl, and shouted her name. She recognized the guy, and they embraced in a warm hug. James was in shock— not because of the way his girlfriend and the man hugged, but because he had never heard a man scream that way before. The other guys came over and began taking selfies with Kelly while James watched them have fun. Kelly was so caught up in the moment that she forgot James was watching her. She stopped taking pictures with the guys and explained who they were. "They were the male cheerleaders at my old high school. I haven't seen them since graduation." She then introduced them to James, and they all stood around laughing and joking for a few minutes.

One of the guys suddenly said, "Hey, I know your face from somewhere, James. I just can't place it."

"It must be from television. I was always on the local networks in high school."

"Yeah. That must be it," the man agreed.

Not too long after joking around and laughing some more, the group went their separate ways. As soon as James and Kelly made it to the car, some couples were walking by who also remembered Kelly from high school. All of them took selfies with her, too. When they finished, Kelly saw that James was smiling. "I admit that I did not believe you when you said you were that popular." Kelly laughed as she got into the passenger's side of the car after he opened the door for her. They drove away, laughing and joking about the night's events.

****

Back at the lounge, everyone was having fun. The lounge was one of few attractions in the small city. Everyone loved going there because there were never any issues. Top Shelf was one of three lounges in the city, but it was the biggest one and the only one that had an expensive cover charge, which was a good value because of the price of the drinks and the atmosphere.

The owner of Top Shelf was a rich, retired professional basketball player named Nick. Although not famous, he did play professionally for a long time. He wanted to develop a serious relationship with Chelsea, but she kept avoiding the commitment. Tiffany often told her, "You need to stop playing with that man, girl. If I had the opportunity to marry a good man who was as successful as Nick, I wouldn't hesitate!"

As Nick walked throughout the lounge with his bodyguards always nearby, he went to the table where Jason and the ladies sat. All the ladies knew Nick well because he and Chelsea had been hit-and-miss with developing a relationship

She's Ready at 18... He's Ready at 38!

for over two years. Chelsea never committed to getting serious because she thought he could never be faithful to one woman since so many women were always after him. Nick took a seat at the table with them and said, "The next round's on me!" He then saluted Jason and winked at Chelsea.

Even though she did not want a relationship with Nick, Chelsea was extremely attracted to him. Every other time he approached her, he never asked her to dance, but that night he did—and she did not refuse. She was in a good mood, and something seemed different about him at that moment. As they danced, he told her his life changed, and he felt like a new man. She smiled because she believed it was just another attempt to win her over. "What about your life has changed?" she asked.

"I gave my life to Christ and recently completed a discipleship course at the church," he said with great joy.

"Which church?"

"Grace Church."

Chelsea stopped dancing and walked over to Jason, who was one of the leaders at that church. "Is it true that Nick completed the discipleship course at the church?"

Jason smiled, pulled out his phone, and showed Chelsea a picture of people holding certificates on a stage. He zoomed in on the image to show her Nick holding his Certificate of Completion.

Suddenly, the music stopped, and Chelsea noticed the spotlight was placed on her. Jason slowly backed away because he saw that Nick had walked up behind her. As she turned around, Nick got on one knee and asked, "Chelsea, will you marry me?"

She was in shock and asked, "Why are you doing this?"

"Chelsea, I believe you are the woman I will spend the rest of my life with. If you do not believe the same thing, then say so."

Chelsea smiled as she looked around, noticing that everyone in the lounge was looking at them. She also noticed they were on all the big screens scattered throughout. When she began crying, Nick asked her one more time. The tears really started to flow at that point — and she said, "Yes, Nick! Yes! Yes! Yes!" Everyone simultaneously started clapping and shouting congratulatory words. Chelsea stretched out her hand, Nick placed the ring on her finger, and the revelers busted out into another roar.

Nick and Chelsea had been on numerous dates but never got serious because she did not trust him to protect her heart. When he said he became a Christian and had completed the discipleship course, it was like a dream come true because she had made up in her mind that she would not settle again for just having any man in her life.

The newly engaged couple walked out of the lounge holding hands. When they were seated in Nick's luxury SUV, he gave her some more news. "I'm selling the lounge and took a position on the ministerial staff at Grace Church."

Chelsea's tears seemed to be flowing nonstop. "I prayed and asked God for a husband who was in the ministry because I, too, am about to take that step," she said.

"I always wanted to be in church but struggled throughout my life because I did not want to pull away from the lifestyle I loved and the people who surrounded me. This is the best decision I have ever made. I do not regret it one bit." As they excitedly talked about their plans, they agreed to go through marriage counseling and to remain celibate until their wedding night. "Where would you like to go right now? Anywhere. Your choice."

"A walk on the pier would be great," she replied.

Nick instructed the driver to take them to the main fishing pier, which was not only a tourist spot, but it was also the first place the two went on their first date.

****

Back at the lounge, Sarah was smiling at Jason because she was impressed with how he was helping to change the lives of men older than him.

"My dad and other Elders do most of the work. I'm still learning how to facilitate like the others in the discipleship ministry," Jason said. "Are you ready to go? If so, I'd like to walk you to your car."

As they stood and prepared to leave, Tiffany shouted, "I'm not going to be the only friend left behind in this lounge!" so she left with Sarah and Jason. When they made it to the parking garage, Jason walked Tiffany to her car first and opened the driver's side door for her. Once inside, she rolled down her window, smiled at the couple, and told Sarah, "I hope Jason becomes a great friend." Before driving off, she winked her eye at Sarah.

Jason then walked Sarah to her car and opened her driver's side door. Before getting in, she gazed into his eyes and then embraced for a few seconds. Jason was 6'5," and Sarah was 5'5". She enjoyed looking up to him because she had never hugged a man that tall before.

"I can tell you're exhausted, Sarah. Would you like for me to follow you home to make sure you get home safely?"

She smiled broadly when she said, "Yes. I would appreciate that very much." Inside her head, Sarah is screaming for joy. Jason gently closed her door then walked to his truck. She watched him get in and pull up behind her, and he followed her to her house.

Chapter Two: Friends

The next day, Sarah received a phone call that woke her up out of her sleep. She gathered her thoughts and realized it was Chelsea calling.

"You know, I bet Tiffany that you would be the first one to leave with a guy. I lost the bet but heard you left with someone, too," Chelsea stated.

Sarah remembered the previous night's events and smiled. She then looked across her bedroom and saw Jason still sleeping on the couch in the lounge area of her room. She started getting a little stressed out because she had a daughter, and she prided herself on setting an excellent example for young women. She hung up the phone and proceeded to wake up Jason.

At first, he forgot where he was. When she questioned him about what happened between them last night, he assured her nothing happened, even though she passed out no sooner than her head hit the pillow. Sarah was astonished that Jason did not take advantage of her vulnerable state and began to relax. After all, her body would have let her know if something happened, especially after being celibate for ten years.

"Listen," Jason said, "I was raised by a great man who taught me how to treat a woman." His words and voice calmed her, and they enjoyed a great conversation while Jason massaged her feet. During their chat, he stated, "I repositioned one of your security cameras in the upstairs hallway to zoom in on the bedroom area. Let's go and have a look at the feed."

The video showed Jason laying Sarah in her bed and him immediately walking out of the bedroom. After watching that part of the video, Sarah embraced Jason and told him, "I really appreciate you being the man you are." She was also amazed that he was mindful enough to reposition the camera to record everything that showed the innocence of his actions.

They laughed and joked around, all while learning they had a lot in common and loved doing many of the same things. While they were talking, Asia walked into the room. Sarah was embarrassed about his presence at first because she always tried to set a good example for her daughter, and she didn't know how his being there would impact Asia.

"Everything is alright, mom," Asia quickly stated. "I spoke with Jason last night after you passed out on the couch. After he picked you up and brought you into your bedroom, I made sure you were properly tucked in your bed."

Once again, they watched the security camera footage, which confirmed all that Asia stated. Another recording they viewed showed Jason going to the couch and Asia talking to him for about 30 minutes before she left the room.

Asia was comfortable speaking with Jason because she had met him at a collaborative Vacation Bible School (VBS) a year prior. As she explained that to her mother, Sarah became even more overjoyed because of the bond developing between Asia and Jason. She was even more relieved to know Jason wasn't a complete stranger to her daughter. Sarah looked up toward the sky and smiled, thanking God for piecing it all together. Asia then left the bedroom to give her mother and Jason their privacy.

****

Once alone, Jason and Sarah stared at each other and smiled. Sarah broke the silence by saying, "Please explain the reason why you are single." He paused for a moment, took one of her hands in his, and continued staring into her eyes. He was speechless but calm. "Go ahead, Jason. Say what needs to be said."

He then clinched both of her hands and explained in four words: "I am a virgin." He paused to get her reaction. When he didn't see a change in her demeanor, he continued. "I am embarrassed about it at times, which is why I hesitated on telling you."

Sarah squeezed his hands and replied with the gentlest tone, "It's okay." While Jason continued talking, Sarah smiled and silently thanked God for sending Jason to her.

"So, please explain why you are single," Jason prompted.

"I have been happily single for ten years. In that time, I have been able to spend more time with Asia. The only long-term relationship I ever had was with her father, and that ended when she was a baby."

They both stated they were afraid to get into relationships because of past incidents and agreed not to rush into what seemed to be a relationship developing between them. Sarah had been hoping the right man would show up in her life, and there Jason was—sitting on the edge of her bed, rubbing her feet. Jason smiled as he silently gazed into her eyes. "Why are you looking at me like that?" Sarah asked.

Jason stood, took her by the hand to pull her into a warm embrace, and then whispered in her ear, "I believe you are the dream woman who is going to be my reality."

"Why do you say that?" Sarah asked as she started blushing in obvious excitement.

"Well, I must admit that I have seen you before at the lounge but always thought you had a husband because you are so beautiful."

"Hopefully, that will change in the future, and I will have a husband," she replied shyly.

Moments later, Jason's cell phone rang. "I must take this. It's my dad calling." He answered the phone, had a brief talk with his father, then let Sarah know his dad wanted to have a father-son breakfast.

That brought a smile to Sarah's face because she knew it was good to see a father and son still have those types of outings together. "Tell me a little about your father, Jason."

Jason spoke with obvious pride. "My dad is Pastor Williams of Grace Church on the north side of town," he began. Sarah smiled at that because she remembered allowing Asia to attend VBS at that church. Jason continued. "My father is known as a great man of God throughout the city because the church is always helping the community and has an excellent children's ministry. He's most known for writing many books that help in mentoring men." Sarah was thoroughly impressed. All that Jason said highlighted the fact that he had a strong foundation—something that would surely help him as he continued to grow in life. "Although my family is living well now, there was a time when we were seriously struggling. My dad used to work at a convenience store for over 20 years but left that job to become a pastor. Our family and a few others started the first church, which was located in a renovated building. Through the years, the congregation grew to over 2,000 members within six months during a recession. A few members of the first church believed in my father's vision, so they invested in building the current church from the ground up. Needless to say, to accommodate the growth, the current church is double the size of the original one." He paused and seemed to go into deep thought before saying, "Honestly, we're not overly excited about the size of the new building as much as we are overjoyed by the hundreds of volunteers from the church who help with and support community events, which is why the mayor also loves Grace Church." Jason and Sarah talked for a few more minutes before Jason said, "It's about time that I head home."

While walking to the front door, they stopped to embrace in a long, loving hug. When they separated, both immediately noticed Asia looking at them in awe. She hadn't seen her mother that happy in a very long time. As she walked over to say goodbye to Jason, he addressed both of them. "I would love to cook dinner for you sometime this week." Sarah was speechless and Asia, smiling, replied with a simple, "Sure! Thank you, Minister Jason!"

Once out of sight, Sarah closed the door and turned to her daughter with a huge smile on her face. "Mom, your wait might be over," Asia stated with a bit of confidence.

Just then, Asia's cell phone rang. It was her father, James. He called to ask if she wanted to have lunch with him later, to which she agreed. He had been back in town for a few weeks and made it a point to spend as much time as possible with his daughter.

While Asia talked to her dad, Sarah received a call from Chelsea, who was relaxing at home, sitting on her bed. Chelsea was still excited about being proposed to the night before. She was single and had never been married, so she asked Sarah to give her some pointers as she prepared for marriage. "Since it's too late for a Saturday morning breakfast, how about we meet for lunch to talk about it?" Sarah suggested.

"Sounds like a plan. Let me ask you something first: Would you do me the honor of being my Maid of Honor?"

Sarah screamed into the phone, "Yes! I would be honored!" She had been a Maid of Honor a few times already and absolutely loved the responsibilities that go along with the title. They agreed on a place and time and said their goodbyes. As Sarah hung up the phone, she noticed Asia looking at her and smiling again. She told her daughter what happened at the lounge when Nick proposed to Chelsea and that she was just asked to be Chelsea's Maid of Honor. Asia got excited for her mother and told her she would make an awesome Maid of Honor. They embrace excitedly and then walk upstairs while holding hands, talking about marriage in general, and discussing Asia's upcoming lunch with her father.

****

A few hours later, Sarah and Chelsea meet up at a local restaurant. As they were going over the initial phases of wedding planning, Chelsea tells Sarah she selected Tiffany as her Matron of Honor, just as Tiffany entered and was making her way to their table.

"Why are you just mentioning this to me now?" Sarah whispered. She turns all the way around and sees Tiffany approaching with teary eyes and a stressed-out look on her face. As she got closer, she started crying loudly. Sarah and Chelsea stand and hug Tiffany to console her before helping her to an empty seat at the table. The waiter came over and asked if they wanted to go into the empty party room, to which Sarah stated, "Thank you. I think that may be best."

Once in the room, Tiffany calmed down a bit and told her friends why she was crying. "My daughter, Sophia, told me she is pregnant by a professor at her college. To make matters worse, the professor is married, and his wife doesn't have children, nor is she capable of having them." Sarah and Chelsea were shocked by the news but instantly became incredibly angry. Tiffany started crying again and, through the tears and sobbing, said, "Sophia is convinced the professor is going to leave his wife for her and the baby. I'll tell you this: I want to ruin that man's career because he has ruined my daughter's college dreams!"

"Please, Tiffany. Try to think rationally here and consider your actions before doing anything," Sarah suggested. Chelsea, however, agreed with Tiffany, and they began to argue with Sarah. When she had enough of being ganged up on, Sarah stood and, with a loud voice, told them both, "Stop it! Will you calm down and consider the wife, the baby, and Sophia? Get out of your feelings for just a moment!"

At that time, Sophia walked into the room. Her presence shocked all three women into silence. "I really want to be strong while going through this and need to talk to all three of you about it," Sophia said. "I knew my mom was coming here to meet you, so I followed her here." All three ladies remained speechless, so Sophia found that the perfect opportunity to tell more of her story. "The professor didn't pursue me, so please get that thought out of your head. Our relationship actually started through a chain of strange events."
The women continued looking at her with no facial expression that acknowledged they understood. Instead, looks of frustration fell over their faces.

"His name is Professor Wilkins. He is 27 years old and one of the youngest professors on campus. All of the students love his Psychology classes, and the other professors love him, too. He is also an Assistant Basketball Coach and owns a few businesses."

Sophia paused to see if her mother or the other ladies had any response. They said nothing, so she continued.

"Since I tutor a lot of students, the college gave me access to the professors' lounge area. One day, I walked in and noticed Professor Wilkins in the back with his head on the table. He was crying, so I asked if everything was okay. He told me right away that he didn't want to talk about it but thanked me for asking before getting up and walking out. I tutor on Mondays, Wednesdays, and Fridays, and each day I entered the lounge, he would be in that same spot doing the same thing: crying. I left him alone for a week, but when I saw him crying again, I spoke to him and just encouraged him, letting him know that whatever it was, everything would be alright. He was speechless, so I asked him to please tell me what was going on. He paused for a long time while staring at me, and then the tears began to flow more heavily when he told me that his wife was frustrated with him because he couldn't get her pregnant. He said she was convinced it was a problem with him not impregnating her, so she started having an affair with her fertility doctor. Professor Wilkins found out about the affair through one of his wife's friends and learned she has been cheating on him for over a year and even moved out of the house. Despite his efforts to try and work things out between them, she filed for divorce after being separated for 12 months. He told me that he hurts because he never wanted to dissolve his marriage as it gets closer to finalizing the divorce. I encouraged him some more, and shortly afterward, he got up from his seat and walked away. After that encounter, I told him I would check on him periodically. He insisted that I don't and said he would like it if I forgot everything he told me.

  He didn't return to the lounge for over a week. One day, I saw him at a coffee shop on campus. He looked normal, so I stopped in and spoke to him. He seemed genuinely happy to see me and told me he finally realized there was nothing he could do about his situation, so he was going to keep pressing on with his life. For some reason, I smiled and then reached out to hug him. He didn't hug me back right away, as he seemed somewhat paralyzed by my actions, but he finally chose to embrace me, too and thanked me for being concerned. Before leaving the coffee shop that day, he asked me to have lunch with him. The shop has a snack area, so we sat in there, ate lunch, and had an awesome two-hour conversation.

I told him I had to go because I was meeting Lizzie and Asia for dinner later that Saturday night. He walked me to my car and, before I got in, we embraced each other again. He then pulled back, looked at me, and then just froze in place with a strange facial expression. He told me he must stay away from me because he liked me, was still legally married, and was a professor at my college. He knew I liked him, too, so we agreed not to meet again until he was divorced.

A few months passed, and I ran into him again in the school's lounge. I literally bumped into him, and my books fell to the floor. He helped me pick them up, and once we stood, we kissed. From that point on, we kept seeing each other. We honestly had sex one time and, eventually, I found out I was pregnant. I didn't tell anyone at first because I was too embarrassed." Sophia turned to look directly at her mother. "That's why I haven't been home in months, mom. I was a virgin, and that's how I know he is my baby's father. I told him about the baby the same day I told you. He started crying and was speechless at first, but he was happy. I thought his reaction was odd until he explained how he always wanted a baby, but his wife couldn't give him one. He then said he wants to do the right thing and marry me before the baby is born, but he is still waiting for his divorce to be finalized. The baby will be here in four months, though." Sophia stopped talking and allowed all of what she said to soak into her mother's and friends' minds.

The trio of women was speechless. At first, all of them thought it was one of those situations where a young lady was breaking up a happy home because of an irresponsible professor who took advantage of a student, but they were all wrong. Due to his age and pending divorce, they were at ease but insisted on meeting him. Sophia knew they would want that, so she had already called and asked him to come to the restaurant and to wait for her to call him in.

"He's already here?" Sarah asked.

"Yes. He's in the restaurant's dining area." Sophia left the room to get him and, when they came in, the women noticed he carried a folder in his hand. They were left speechless yet again because they did not expect to meet him so quickly. The three ladies were also captivated by his stature and handsomeness, which helped them understand why Sophia fell for him so fast and why she didn't mind the eight-year age difference.

As he approached the table, none of the ladies smiled. They wanted to but chose to present a displeasing environment against him instead. It was amazing to see all of them on one accord as if their reaction was rehearsed. It showed they were truly in tune with one another. "Hello, ladies. I am Professor Wilkins. I understand why you are not pleased with me." As he continued talking, Sarah cut him off midsentence and asked about his pending divorce. He handed her the folder, which contained court documents that outlined the legal separation from his wife.

As Sarah read through the documents, she saw that the divorce should be final within the next seven days. She then grabbed the card with Professor Wilkins' lawyer's number and stepped away to call him. Since she was a lawyer, too, she knew who his legal representative was on a professional level.

Professor Wilkins walked over to Sophia and, as they embraced, he rubbed her belly while gazing lovingly into her eyes. The other ladies watched them and were in awe to see them interact as they did.

Sarah returned to the room and shared with them what the professor's lawyer told her. "He explained that Professor Wilkins' wife abandoned him, filed for divorce after 12 months of separation, and shortly after, she was arrested and has been incarcerated for the past 11 months for assaulting another woman on that other woman's property. As it turned out, that other woman was also having an affair with the fertility doctor. Apparently, the doctor has a habit of lying to women about their fertility results, convincing many that their husbands were the problem, which is precisely what he did to the professor and his wife."

Professor Wilkins was shocked by that report because he didn't know other victims received erroneous test results. However, he quickly regrouped because he remembered his wife telling him she had only married him for his looks and money during one of their arguments.

Sarah quickly summed up the rest of the story. "Professor Wilkin's soon-to-be ex-wife received a one-year sentence and is suing the fertility doctor." After that thorough update, the ladies no longer had a negative perception of Professor Wilkins.

Professor Wilkins could see the women were dazed, so he asked Sarah to return his folder to him. After receiving it, he told them he wanted to take Sophia to her mother's house and that he would be returning to his own. He explained he gave his soon-to-be ex-wife the home and a car and that he was living in a condominium until he and Sophia could officially move in together after his divorce was final. Once again, his words left the ladies dumbfounded. Before leaving, Sophia joyfully hugged her mother and then waved as the couple walked out of the restaurant hand-in-hand.

****

After Sophia and Professor Wilkins left the restaurant, the friends looked back and forth at one another, smiling and relieved. They then started talking about the baby.

She's Ready at 18… He's Ready at 38!

While in conversation, Asia's dad called Sarah. He wanted to know Asia's favorite color. Sarah paused for a moment before answering him because she got upset that he forgot their daughter's favorite color. "Purple. Her favorite color is purple." He thanked her and quickly hung up the phone. Sarah called him right back, but he didn't answer because his phone was on silent at the time.

"Is everything alright?" Chelsea asked.

"Yes. James is just trying to reclaim time with his daughter." Moments later, her phone rings again. It was James calling back.

"I'm sorry for missing your call. Thanks again for giving me Asia's favorite color. I asked because I'm going to buy her some purple roses. I know she's going to love them."

Sarah smiled and replied, "Enjoy your time together. Bye for now."

****

James arrived at the flower shop to purchase his daughter a dozen purple roses. When he got in line to pay, he noticed Dave was in line ahead of him. Between the two men stood an extremely attractive, professionally dressed woman. Dave turned around and saw the woman and James staring at him simultaneously. James noticed Dave had two houseplants in his hands and laughed at him.

"Why are you laughing?" Dave asked.

"Those are old-people plants, man!"

Dave laughed, too, and said, "These plants are not for an old person. They are for a loving person."

The woman chimed in. "I love those types of plants because they don't die fast like roses and some other flowers do." She then complimented Dave on his choices, which prompted James to hide his roses behind his back when she turned in his direction.

After Dave paid for his purchase, he waited for the lady and walked with her out of the store. He glanced back at James and smiled as the woman walked through the door he held open for her. Dave didn't walk her to her car, though. The two went in opposite directions, but not before he thanked her for her kind words.

As James walked to his SUV with the dozen purple roses nicely gift wrapped for Asia, he noticed he was parked next to the woman he saw in the store. When he spoke to her, she seemed both surprised and pleased.

"Do you know Dave?" she asked.

"Yes. I know him well. He was a poor kid growing up, and he often looked up to me because I was successful."

The woman told James, "You should be looking up to him now since he's a millionaire."

James was taken aback. He had no idea Dave was a millionaire! "How do you know that about him?"

"Well, Dave owns a small Information Technology company that services all of the major companies in the city. He is always on television and seen with celebrities when they come to the city," she replied, obviously knowing she knew something James did not.

James was silent and amazed as the woman spoke because he never pictured Dave growing up to be famous. She also told him that Dave had been single for a long time, had no children, and almost every single woman in the city wanted him. The two ended up getting into a lengthy conversation before James remembered Asia was waiting for him. He thanked the lady for the exchange and then hurried to his SUV so that he could rush to see his daughter.

She's Ready at 18... He's Ready at 38!

****

When James showed up to meet Asia, he saw her talking to a man. He walked up to the pair, and Asia introduced her friend, DJ, to her father. James looked puzzled and slightly angered. "Dad, why are you looking at him like that?"

"He looks like a man my age!"

Asia and DJ burst out laughing, which only made James angrier. "Practically everyone who sees DJ for the first time thinks he's much older than he is, mostly because of his beard. Dad, DJ is the same age as me! We have been great friends since junior high school."

James gave DJ a slight smirk and then started questioning DJ, which was standard for a father to do. DJ wasn't at all intimidated and actually enjoyed the question-answer period. "What do the initials DJ stand for?"

"Dave Jacobson, sir."

"Hmm... I don't know anyone in town with the last name Jacobson." DJ smiled at that comment because almost everyone tells him the same thing. In a town their size, it seemed everyone knows everyone. They continued talking about various topics until DJ said he had to get back to work. "What is it that you do?" James asked.

"I manage a restaurant." He said his goodbyes and, as he walked away, James noticed his daughter smiling at DJ, who then looked back and winked his eye at her. James caught the exchange between the two and laughed because he remembered 'the wink' he used to give women as he walked away from them.

"So, tell me more about DJ."

Asia told her father that his parents moved out of town as soon as he graduated, which was why he lived alone and managed the restaurant. "Dad, DJ is an awesome, mature guy."

As she spoke, James felt within his heart that Asia was in love with DJ, but he wasn't yet convinced that he was the right one for his daughter. He maintained his cool, though, because he didn't want to upset her. "When DJ gets off work, we're going to the mall."

"He seems like a good guy."

Asia nodded the affirmative and smiled broadly...again.

"It must be tough growing up without his dad..." Before he could finish his sentence, his cell phone rang. It was one of his friends, but James declined the call knowing his friend could be long-winded. He shot him a quick text to let him know he would call him back shortly.

His friend replied: "I'm on the way out of town for a few weeks but wanted to let you know that a reliable source told me Dave is in a relationship with Asia."

James replied: "I know. I'm dealing with it right now!" His friend didn't respond immediately, so he thought the texting session was done. He smiled because he appreciated having friends who go the extra mile for him.

His friend eventually replied: "Okay. Let me know if you need my help when I get back in town..."

James read the beginning of the text but stopped and deleted the messages by mistake as he was trying to turn off the notifications on his phone. He didn't receive any other texts, so he focused on spending quality time with his daughter. "How's Lizzie doing?" he asked.

Asia smiled because she desperately wanted to talk to her dad about Lizzie and Ricky. She explained all that happened between Lizzie, Ricky, and the incident with the sheriff. "Dad, how do you really feel about their relationship?"

James paused before answering. "Well, since Lizzie is of age, then everyone should respect her decision." Asia said she agreed with his view. The father-daughter team then continued enjoying the rest of their outing without any further interruptions.

Chapter Three: Secrets

Ricky and Lizzie had been secretly meeting, but that's been it. They were quite fond of each other but would not consider taking it to the next level until they overcame particular hurdles. The age difference was not an issue to overcome. Still, Ricky was about to make a major business decision that would require Lizzie deciding if she was going to transfer to another university. He was a respectable man and loved by many throughout the city because he was always helping the community somehow.

Even though the community loved him, that didn't mean his latest actions were accepted by everyone, especially Lizzie's parents. They really wanted her to transfer to the university that offered her a full scholarship, which also meant she would be away from Ricky.

Ever since the day after the incident at Lizzie's house, Ricky had been under fire from his friends and friends of Lizzie's parents. Word had quickly spread about what happened, and he couldn't go anywhere without someone giving him a nasty look. They treated him as if he were a rapist, mainly because most of them wouldn't accept that he could legally have a relationship with an 18-year-old. Fortunately for Lizzie, she was only home periodically on the weekends from a prep college, so she didn't have to experience contact with people who would've most likely openly judged her, too.

****

A week after the incident, Lizzie decided to head home to spend time with her parents. She called her mother to let her know she was coming home, at which time they discussed having a mother-daughter lunch at the house. "If your dad doesn't have to work, we'll have lunch at one of the local restaurants like we normally do," her mother stated.

On Saturday morning, when Lizzie arrived, she had a quick moment to see her dad before he left for work. She opened the door and walked in on her parents hugging in the kitchen. Her dad was the first to notice her, and he was thrilled to see her. She was excited to see him, too, especially since he didn't seem to be mad regarding the incident a week prior. She thought he would be unapproachable, but he conducted himself as if nothing ever happened. When they embraced, her dad said, "Welcome home! I love you!"

"I love you, too, dad!" He then helped her bring her bags into the house. "Thanks for your help. I hope you have a great day!" As her dad left the house smiling, she saw that her mom was smiling as well. "Why is dad so happy and not mad at me?"

"He has chosen to put it all behind him. He trusts that you will make the correct decisions in life," her mother replied. Lizzie smiled and assured her mother that she would, indeed, do just that.

Lizzie followed her mother into the kitchen to help prepare her favorite meal for lunch. While there, she hugged her mother and told her she was so happy to have a mother like her. In turn, Olivia told her she is the luckiest mother to have such an awesome daughter and that she loved her so much. "Is there anything, in particular, you want to talk about?" Olivia asked. Lizzie smiled because she was expecting her mother to question her about Ricky. Olivia, however, remembered from a class during a women's conference not to be aggressive with her daughter when having conversations regarding relationships. The intent should be not to pressure young women because being aggressive could push them away to places they need not go.

Before Lizzie could tell her mother what she wanted to talk about, her mother received a call from her husband. "I made it to work 20 minutes early and wanted to talk to you for a few minutes before going in," he said. He didn't know at the time that his wife and daughter had already started eating lunch. Olivia walked out of the sunroom laughing and smiling as her husband told her a few jokes.

Since Olivia was on the phone with her husband, Lizzie took advantage of the opportunity to call Ricky. He answered on the first ring and was excited to hear her voice. "I only have a few minutes to talk because I'm still at lunch with my mom." When she told him she noticed he answered the phone so quickly, it left him speechless.

Eventually, he told her, "I was just thinking about spending more time with you right before you called. I'm at the pet resort waiting for my dog, sitting on a bench, thinking about us." They talked for a few minutes more and then agreed to meet for dinner that night. "I need your input regarding a business decision," he stated.

"Really? Let's talk about it now!" she said excitedly.

"Okay. I am considering buying Top Shelf from Nick. After getting engaged to Chelsea, he wants to sell the lounge as part of his lifestyle change. He asked me to buy it from him because he knows I'm an honest businessman and would not change how the lounge is currently operating," he explained. Ricky already owned a few businesses but owning a lounge had been his dream. "I would love it if you would help me manage it, especially since you are majoring in business."

"Yes, Ricky! Yes! Yes! Yes!" Then, she paused, remembering she is still a full-time college student. "I'm sorry. I need some time to consider that opportunity. Committing to such a thing would drastically change the course of my current plans."

"I would think it's right up your alley, especially since you're majoring in Business Management."

Lizzie frowned. She had already committed to attending college out of the state but hadn't shared those details with Ricky yet, so she told him right then. He told her he understood and that if she did go away to college, she would always have a position in the lounge as the General Manager. Lizzie smiled because she wasn't expecting Ricky to ask her to assist him in the future. After they talked for a few more minutes, Lizzie asked Ricky if he would consider moving to the city where she would be going to college.

Without hesitation, he said, "I would gladly move to that city to be with you, as long as I have someone dependable to manage my business for me." The two decided to discuss everything that night at dinner. While they were talking, someone at the dog parlor called Ricky's name over the speaker, letting him know his dog was ready for pick up. "Oh. Before I go, I must tell you I have another surprise for you tonight."

"Tell me now! Stop teasing me!"

"Nope! I'm not giving in to you again. See you tonight."

After they hung up from their call, Lizzie could not keep from smiling. When her mother returned, Lizzie told her about the conversation with Ricky. Outwardly, Olivia smiled. Inwardly, she was angry. It was hard to maintain her composure, so she excused herself and went to the bathroom. When she closed the bathroom door, she stretched her hands to the sky and let out a silent scream before gathering her thoughts and returning to the table with her daughter.

****

Olivia and Lizzie talked about other things and enjoyed the rest of their afternoon. Lizzie then told her mother she needed to take a nap. After they embraced, she called Ricky while walking to her room. "Are you busy?"

"Yes. I'm talking to Nick about the upcoming meeting to review the paperwork for purchasing the lounge."

"Okay. We'll talk again later," Lizzie stated.

That night, they met for dinner at a restaurant in a neighboring city since Ricky wasn't a pleasant sight for anyone in their own. While they were enjoying dinner, Nick and Chelsea came to their table. Lizzie was embarrassed because she didn't think Chelsea would approve of her relationship.

"It's okay, Lizzie. I don't know a better guy than him who would ensure your happiness," Chelsea said with sincerity.

Nick then placed a folder on the table. Within was the purchasing documentation and other papers that ensured the property was in good condition. Ricky asked Lizzie and Chelsea to review the documents. Since both were majoring in Business, he knew they would have experience reviewing paperwork similar to what was in the folder. The ladies stepped away from the table and walked over to an open one to review the documents. While the ladies did that, Nick and Ricky talked about the lounge. After their review, they returned and made some recommendations that amazed the men.

"I have no problem modifying the paperwork if you want me to, Ricky," Nick stated. Ricky readily agreed to the recommendations while gazing at Lizzie.

Chelsea purposely interrupted the gazing session and asked Lizzie if she would like to accompany her to the restroom, which she did. Once in the restroom, Chelsea immediately asked Lizzie to tell her about her relationship with Ricky.

She's Ready at 18... He's Ready at 38!

"Ricky didn't pursue me, if that's what you're thinking. He was actually trying to stay away from me, but we kept crossing paths in the weirdest places. Most often, it was at events he hosted or was a guest speaker." Chelsea seemed satisfied with her response, so they returned to the table.

When they made it back to the guys, they noticed Nick was crying. "Why are you crying?" Chelsea asked.

"It is an amazing feeling to finally have the right woman," he replied. Chelsea was speechless. She had never seen a man cry because of love. She walked up to him, and they held each other.

While they were in a loving embrace, Lizzie and Ricky stared at each other. "Is that how you feel about me?" she asked him.

"Yes, Lizzie. It is."

"Then why aren't you crying?"

Ricky was dumbfounded for a moment before stating, "Because Nick is more sensitive than I am." Lizzie started laughing. "Why are you laughing? Did I miss the joke?"

"I'm laughing because I knew you would come up with some crazy reply!" While they were laughing, they noticed Nick and Chelsea staring at them.

Nick commented, "Y'all look like you've been together for years!"

Shortly after, Chelsea's brother, Chris, came to their table to speak to everyone. Although not everyone knew Chris was her brother, they did know him as the restaurant's manager. He was rather popular because people loved his hospitality. He was highly paid and sought after by many large restaurants. Everyone at the table was happy to see Chris, except for Ricky. After he engaged his sister and the others in conversation, he walked away while having an intense stare-down with Ricky, which Chelsea witnessed. "May I speak to you outside for a moment?" she asked Ricky. As they walked out the door, Chris saw them and followed them outside.

When the three of them were together, Ricky looked at Chris and said, "James is back in town. I think you owe him an apology."

"Apology for what?" Chelsea asked.

Ricky remained silent and stared at Chris, waiting for him to respond. After a few moments of deafening silence, Chris told Chelsea the story, all while looking directly at her because he refused to look Ricky in the eye.

"While we were in high school, there was a party that many of us attended on the local college campus. Everyone had fun, and there was a point when James passed out from being drunk. Before he passed out, he was in a room with a young lady, but I and some other friends were staring and laughing at him when he woke up. As we walked out of the room, I turned to James and said, 'Thank you.' At the time, people thought I was a homosexual, but that wasn't true. The whole thing started as a joke on a drunk friend, but James chased us down and beat me pretty badly. I pressed charges, and when we went to court, James pleaded guilty. The agreement was that James would leave the city instead of going to jail. James was never told it was a joke because everyone who knew about it was too afraid to tell him. They thought they would get a beatdown, too."

Before Chris even finished telling the story, Chelsea was in tears. "You have no idea…you do not understand the impact of your decision to play that joke on James, Chris. At the time, James had a daughter and was engaged to Sarah. That joke separated a father from his daughter and prevented a marriage from happening!"

"Chelsea, I've been trying to get my life in order," Chris cried aloud. "I've been a faithful member of the church. I'm engaged to be married and have a son who will be born in two months. Can you please call Sarah so that I can explain to her what really happened?"

"Sure," she said. She called Sarah and asked her, "Are you alone?"

"Yes, I am," Sarah replied.

"My brother has something he needs to tell you."

"Okay. Put Chris on the phone."

Chris explained everything that happened that night at the party. As he shared every detail, tears fell from Sarah's eyes. "Please accept my apology, Sarah. Please forgive me. I didn't know…"

"I thought James left the city because of me…" Her voice trailed off when her doorbell rang. She saw through the security system's camera that Jason was at her door. She unlocked the door and spoke through the intercom system for him to come into the study. When Jason walked into the study, she gestured that she was on the phone, so he sat on the chaise lounge and started flipping through a magazine. Before she turned her attention back to Chris, she wrote on a piece of paper who she was talking to and handed it to Jason. "Yes, Chris. I forgive you. Please put your sister back on the phone."

Chris handed the phone back to Chelsea, who then tells her friend, "I'm so sorry for bothering you, and I'm sorry for my brother's actions."

Sarah paused for a moment. "Although I am stunned by this information, I am completely over James."

"Thank you for moving on with your life. Focus on Jason. I believe he was specifically created for you."

"I agree, Chelsea," she said while smiling at Jason. He couldn't hear their conversation, but he somehow knew he had something to do with it by the look of love on Sarah's face. She hung up the phone, walked over to the chaise lounge where

Jason was sitting, climbed onto his lap, and told him about her conversation with Chris.

****

Jason wasn't at all fazed by the conversation. Sarah could tell, but she still felt compelled to tell him that she was completely over James. "I wanted to reassure you of that to ensure you know my focus is on the man whose arms I'm in right now."

"Thank you for being honest. I, too, am focused on the woman who's in my arms right now," he said with a smile. "I do, however, have one question. What was the relationship like that you once had with him? I will likely be interacting with him from time to time because of your daughter."

"Well, although we were engaged, his anger issues were the long pole in the tent. Still, I was willing to marry James and overlook those issues because he was genuinely nice to me and treated me like a queen. He was handsome, had a good job, and was starting to get involved in the church. When he first told me he was leaving, I was depressed and hurt deeply because I believed I did everything expected of a good woman. I had convinced myself that another woman had stolen his heart, which further fractured my heart and mind. Until I met you, I never felt comfortable trying to start another serious relationship." As she spoke, she noticed how Jason looked deeply into her eyes. "Please explain your gazing at me."

"I love hearing the sound of your voice. I truly love and appreciate your honesty. I, too, had trouble starting relationships because I was hurt years ago by someone I had proposed to. She left me when she decided she couldn't marry a guy who was into the church as I was because she had other things she wanted to do before committing to the church. That hurt me. I thought she was the perfect woman for me before she said that. She ended up moving out of the state with her sister. She was absolutely sure the man she was going to marry did not live in this city. Not long after relocating, she got married, just as she wanted. I was convinced I would never find someone better than her—until God led me to you." They embraced again and vowed to protect one another's hearts.

Sarah suddenly hopped off Jason's lap, grabbed his hands, and led him to the garage. She showed him a barbeque grill she had there for a few years but never took the time to put it together. Jason took the grill to the back of the house, where both of them spent time piecing it together. "Sarah, I am the happiest I have ever been since I met you. I know you were created just for me." She smiled because that statement just confirmed what Chelsea told her earlier.

Jason mentioned the embarrassment of his virginity at first and reminded Sarah that he wasn't really interested in hanging out with the guys, which was why he was by himself the night they met at Top Shelf. "The real reason I was even there was that I was led to go in my spirit, even though I had been there on a few other occasions."

Sarah could see in his eyes that he was telling the truth. "Honestly, I wasn't interested in being with anyone younger than me, but your intangibles closed the gap." They embraced again until Sarah reminded him they really needed to get the grill put together. Plus, they were trying to take it slow. All of that embracing could lead them down a path neither was ready to take, especially since they just met.

When the grill was just about halfway finished, Sarah received a call from Tiffany. Sarah had forgotten about their scheduled outing, being that she was distracted—in a good way—by Jason. "I'm so sorry, Tiffany!"

"Girl, I am not angry at all. As a matter of fact, I'm on my way to visit one of my male friends!"

"Who? You know you better tell me right now!" Sarah jokingly demanded.

"I can't tell you yet. The time isn't right for me to reveal anything more." They said their goodbyes, and Tiffany went to visit her friend at his job, but only for a few minutes. After she left, she decided to call her daughter to see what her plans were for the rest of the day.

She's Ready at 18... He's Ready at 38!

Chapter Four: The Truth Hurts

Tiffany called Sophia to see if she was free to join her for lunch since Sarah was enjoying her quality time with Jason. Sophia agreed to meet her, and about 15 minutes later, Tiffany notices Professor Wilkins was the one dropping off her daughter. He parked the car, got out, and opened the car door for Sophia. Tiffany smiled at the sweet gesture because she was a woman who appreciated a chivalrous man.

Professor Wilkins walked with Sophia into the restaurant, made quick eye contact with Tiffany, waved at her, and kissed Sophia before returning to his car that was parked near the entrance. She then walked over to her mother, and they embraced for a few seconds. "I'm overjoyed that you are happy, Sophia," Tiffany stated. "I already ordered our food, so it should be out shortly."

While they waited, they reminisced about their previous mother-daughter lunch dates. The conversation took a sudden turn when Sophia asked her mother about her single status. Tiffany smiled and replied, "That's none of your business."

Just as Sophia was about to ask another question, the waiter brought their food to the table. When she looked up at the waiter, she commented that he looked like her father. "He must be a nice guy," he replied with a smile.

"Oh, yes. He is," Sophia replied.

The ladies talked for a while more, then Sophia told her mother she needed to go to the restroom to wash her hands. As she was walking away, Tiffany told the waiter he did, indeed, look like Sophia's father. The two talked for a few minutes more while the waiter placed their plates on the table. Shortly after, he departed to check on the other tables. Tiffany then pulled her hand sanitizer out of her purse and used it because she touched the same menu others before her had touched. The hand sanitizer was a gift from a male friend of hers who worked at another restaurant. When Sophia returned, she immediately noticed the hand sanitizer on the table and that it was labeled with the name of a restaurant she was familiar with. "Mom, where did you get that from?" she asked.

Tiffany smiled slyly and said, "My male friend gave it to me. I'll tell you about him soon." Sophia knew something good was going on, so she asked her mother again about her love life. "Okay, okay, okay! I'm not seeing anyone seriously, but there is a man who is extremely interested in me." She fell silent again, but Sophia wanted to know more. "Listen, before I move forward in any other relationship, I feel it's only right to at least entertain the offer from your father."

Travis was Sophia's father. He never wanted to get married but wanted to come back into their lives and talk about marriage. Travis and Tiffany broke up long ago because she was tired of shacking up. She wanted to do things the right way and in alignment with her belief in God. After years of unhappiness due to his refusal to commit to marriage, they agreed it would be best to separate on good terms. Their relationship was dissolved when Sophia was 12 years old. He has remained an active part of Sophia's life ever since.

Sophia always prayed for her parents to reconnect, so when her mother mentioned possibly getting back with her father, she was overjoyed and began to cry. Tiffany came over and hugged her, and the waiter returned with some extra napkins to wipe the tears away. When the trio noticed the other patrons were staring and smiling at them, the ladies sat down in embarrassment. "Don't be ashamed. There's always something special happening here. Just look around at many of the pictures on the walls." For the first time, the ladies noticed a host of images of various celebrations and, in each, people embraced with smiles and tears. "You see? This restaurant earned its name!" he finished with a smile.

The name of the restaurant was "A Happy Place." Tiffany chose that particular spot because it came highly recommended. Plus, she hadn't been there in the past because it was way on the other side of town.

****

As the moment simmered, Pastor Williams walked up to their table and introduced himself to Sophia. He was already in the restaurant in another room doing a marriage counseling session. He was also the one who recommended A Happy Place to Tiffany. "Are you ready for your session?" he asked.

Sophia was bewildered. She looked at her mom and then threw her hands up in the air as an expression of confusion. Just then, Travis walked up behind her, causing Tiffany to smile widely. "Why are you smiling?"

"Turn around and see why."

As Sophia turned in her chair, she saw her father and started screaming for joy. She jumped out of her seat, hugged her father, and cried tears of joy because she knew her parents were about to receive marriage counseling. "I've often prayed for you and mom to get back together and get married. Hopefully, that is what will happen!" She then turned back around and asked her mom, "Why were you meeting Sarah for lunch if you knew there was going to be a counseling session?"

"Well, Sarah hasn't seen Travis in a long time and wanted to stop by, too. As well, we wanted to keep this a secret as long as possible because the counseling session is to see if we are truly going to move forward." Tiffany didn't really believe they would enter into a relationship again, but she needed to try one more time before moving forward into any other serious relationship.

Travis and Tiffany embraced briefly, but it wasn't an overwhelming embrace, which signaled to Sophia the session might not be fruitful. Still, she was delighted to see her parents at least trying one more time to see if they were meant to be together. When time permitted amid the revelry, Pastor Williams asked them again if they were ready. Travis and Tiffany both said they were.

"What about me?" Sophia asked.

Her dad told her, "I called Professor Wilkins and told him what time to be here to pick you up." She was astonished and looked confused. "I knew about Professor Wilkins the same day your mother found out. I've spoken to him on at least two other occasions since then."

While they were talking, Chelsea and Nick walked out of the room Pastor Williams was just in. Travis, Tiffany, and Sophia were genuinely surprised to see them. Putting two-and-two together, they quickly realized they were the couple who just completed a marriage counseling session. Everyone gave each other hugs, and the pastor reminded Travis and Tiffany about their appointment. Before parting ways, they hug Sophia just as Professor Wilkins entered. He greeted everyone, and then the two couples — he and Sophia, and Nick and Chelsea — leave the restaurant.

Pastor Williams, Travis, and Tiffany head to the private room where the counseling was scheduled to take place. As they prepared to take their seats, Chelsea came back in because she had left her phone behind. She excused herself, grabbed her phone, and left the room. On the way out the door, she looked back and saw that Pastor Williams led the couple in prayer — something he did with each couple before providing counsel. After praying, Chelsea made eye contact with Tiffany. She noticed Tiffany wasn't as happy as she was before going into the room but dismissed it as Tiffany being nervous. She waved at her one more time before closing the door and exiting the restaurant.

****

When Chelsea went outside, she saw Professor Wilkins and Sophia driving away. Nick was waiting at his car to open the door for her. Before she got in, he gave her a big kiss. Once settled in her seat, she reached over and opened his door from the inside. When he got in, he looked at her, smiled, and told her he appreciated her so much, leading to another kiss. "You know, I saw that in a movie once and wanted to make sure I did that for you," she said.

"I saw that same movie, too. Not once has a woman ever reached over to open my door for me," Nick replied. They both paused and then started laughing with joy. Shortly after they drove off, he said, "I have a surprise for you at another location."

Chelsea smiled and said, "Okay!" She then received a call from Sophia.

"Since my mom is busy in her counseling session, I wanted to share some exciting news with someone, so I called you. Are you ready?" Her excitement could be heard clearly through the phone line.

"Yes! Tell me! What is it?"

"On the way to dropping me off, we stopped by the professor's house so that he could check the mail. He received his official divorce decree in the mail today! He was speechless when he realized what it was, so he handed me the paperwork. When I read what it was, I screamed! We are both overjoyed right now and hugged in celebration! He then went into the house to grab some things, so I got back in the car to wait for him. When he came out, he had this huge smile on his face as he walked over to my side of the car. He opened the door, asked me to get back out, and, just as I did, he got on one knee and asked me to marry him! I said yes!!! I am so happy! I wanted to get married but to the right man. I was hoping he was the one. He's on his phone now talking to his parents. He was so excited, too, and wanted to share the good news with them."

While they were still talking, Professor Wilkins got back into the car. Sophia showed him her phone, and he saw that she was talking to Chelsea. He spoke to her briefly, and she replied, "I am happy for both of you. Enjoy your day. I'll check on the two of you later." Nick was silent during all the excitement but then shouted, "Congratulations to you both!"

Shortly after Chelsea and Sophia finished talking, Nick drove into a new housing development composed of expensive estates. They noticed a lot of cars in front of the model home as they walked in to meet the sales representative. After a brief introduction and presentation from the rep, they walked through the house and others that were already built and move-in ready. As they were walking back to the model home, they see Sophia and Professor Wilkins exiting. The couple had decided that they needed to start looking for a home since they were planning to get married. As the two couples met one another again, the ladies embraced, and the guys shook hands.

Before Nick could speak, Professor Wilkins said, "Please, call me Ed."

"Wow, Ed! I see things are moving quite fast for the two of you."

"Yes, they are. Everything is working out perfectly. We hope to close on a house soon." In addition to being a professor, Ed also owned properties, which was how he could afford to purchase one of the estates.

She's Ready at 18… He's Ready at 38!

****

As the ladies continued discussing the joy of the recent changes in their lives, Sophia received a call from Lizzie. She placed the call on speakerphone so that all three of them could talk. Sophia and Chelsea took a few steps away from the guys to continue their conversation with Lizzie. Before Lizzie could tell them the reason for her call, they told her about their life-changing events. Lizzie was extremely happy for them and said, "What perfect timing! I have a relationship question for you and need your advice. Should I stay with Ricky, or should I move on?"

"What sparked that question?" Sophia asked.

Lizzie proceeded to tell them about her visit to a college with her parents. "It was actually my third time visiting the college. While there, I spent more time with this particular guy. He's my age, very mature, and already owns a business. My dad and the guy have already developed a great bond, and my parents know his parents—a wealthy couple. He promised to protect me while I'm there, which really helped his bond with my dad. There's something special about him, and honestly, I like him more than Ricky."

Sophia replied, "I would first suggest you pray about it and go from there. I want you to be happy and make the best decision for yourself. Do your parents know how you feel about the young man at the college?"

"No, they don't. If they did, they would be pressuring me to give him a chance, I'm sure. I really don't know what to say to Ricky because he is such a nice guy. I believe he's practically everything I need in my life, but I'm torn between the two."

When Chelsea spoke, she gave powerful words of wisdom. "Tell him the truth. If he truly cares about you, then he would want what's best for you." Lizzie paused for a few seconds and then agreed to do just that. The ladies said their goodbyes and then returned to enjoy discussing their engagements and coincidental meeting at the model home.

****

While still holding her phone, Lizzie inhaled and exhaled deeply as she prepared to call Ricky. Dialing the number, she felt both nervous and sad because she knew she must do the right thing in her heart. After completing their customary greetings, Lizzie dove right in.

"Ricky, I have decided to transfer to a college out of state."

"That's exciting! I can move to the city with you until you graduate!" he replied.

Before responding to his offer, there was a lengthy pause. "No. I do not want you to move with me." Silence fell over the line again. Ricky became saddened because he was going to proper to her. Lizzie broke the silence. "I think it would be best for both of us if we remain friends going forward and nothing more." That saddened him all the more because he knew he was losing her, but Lizzie wanted first to follow her father's advice to relocate and see what is out there for her before committing to a relationship. "I have to get ready to go now. My parents and I are going to revisit the new college and start decorating my dorm room. Bye, Ricky."

When the call disconnected, Ricky started crying. Little did he know Lizzie was doing the same. Both felt in their hearts that it was over between them. At the time of the call, Lizzie was sitting in her dad's SUV waiting to leave. As soon as she hung up, her mom got in and saw her daughter in tears. "What's wrong, honey? Why are you crying?" Lizzie told her about the conversation she just had with Ricky. "Aww, sweetie. It's natural to feel that way, especially when you really care for someone."

Shortly afterward, her dad gets in. By then, Lizzie had stopped crying, but he could tell something was wrong. He asked her to tell him what was the matter, so she did. He got back out of the SUV and opened her door. When she got out, they embraced. He said to her, "Everything will be alright. I am so proud of you for making your own decision to move on with your life."

They get back into the SUV and, after mom prayed for safe traveling mercies from God, they head to the new school. Along the way, Lizzie sat in the third row of the SUV so that her parents couldn't hear her phone conversations. The first call she made was to Ricky to officially break it off. He was still heartbroken but told her he would always be her friend and that he hoped everything worked out for her. He knew she was going to have an amazing future. That time, when they hung up from the call, both were in good spirits.

After talking to Ricky, Lizzie called Sophia again to tell her the news. Sophia was extremely happy for her because initially, she did not believe Lizzie would make that choice. Everyone thought she was too into Ricky to truly leave him. Still in her overjoyed state about her new direction, she felt the need to share the news with Asia, too. She had not spoken to Asia in a few weeks because she was so consumed with Ricky and school visits. She placed the call and was overjoyed when Asia said she was happy for her. As they continued talking, Lizzie asked Asia to forgive her.

"Forgive you? What for, Lizzie?" Asia asked, obviously confused.

"I've been so excited about sharing my good news and failed to ask if you were busy!"

"Oh, girl. I'm not really busy, but I am about to go out on a special date." Lizzie wanted the details, but Asia refused to speak on it at that moment because she was in a restaurant with her mom and didn't want her to hear. The waitress was also at their table waiting to take their orders, so she had to go.

"Please enjoy your quality time with your mom. We'll touch bases again real soon. Promise," Lizzie stated before they said their goodbyes.

****

Shortly after Asia hung up the phone and they placed their orders, Dave Ferrell joined them at their table. He hugged both ladies but embraced Asia a bit longer. Before they began to talk, Nancy walked up to their table and introduced herself. Asia's mom knew her from high school because they once fought over Asia's dad. Nancy was James' girlfriend before Sarah was. She wanted to tell them that she was part owner of the restaurant and that she would ensure they received the best customer service if they needed any assistance. The entire time she spoke, she looked directly at Sarah. Before departing, she shot Sarah an envious look and then looked at Dave with total contempt. He asked Sarah about Nancy, and Sarah told him the backstory. Asia was in a fit of laughter by the time her mother finished. "Mom, that lady is not in your league!" Dave agreed and gave both Asia and Sarah high-fives across the table.

Sarah continued talking about other run-ins she had with Nancy while they were in school. "I apologize for the interruption, but I have to use the restroom. I'll be right back," Asia stated. Being the consummate gentleman that Dave is, he stood as she departed.

Once seated, Sarah looked him dead in his eyes and said, "You better take excellent care of my daughter. I wrestled with this situation for a while but had to let it go and just be happy for my child."

Dave nodded his understanding, briefly embraced her, and told her, "I will definitely take excellent care of Asia."

Just as they were embracing, Nancy walked by and paused to observe their interaction—and the way Dave rubbed Sarah's back. She thought to herself, "Hmm… They must be a couple." Once in her office, she called James to tell him what she just witnessed.

He grew greatly irritated instantly and became enraged because he still had hatred in his heart for Dave. "Thanks for the information, Nancy," he said before slamming down the phone.

Meanwhile, Asia returned from the restroom and saw her mother and Dave in an embrace, with her mom in tears. She approached and asked, "What's going on here?" Her mom told her about the brief conversation between Dave and her, which prompted Asia to hug her mom as Dave took a seat.

"Asia, I believe Dave is a great man for you. I trust him to take excellent care of you." She turned to address them both. "I'm going to leave now so that you can enjoy yourselves. Don't let me down, Dave." She waved as she walked away with a newfound joy in her heart for her baby girl.

Chapter Five: First Fight

As Nancy made her way back through the restaurant, she noticed Dave sitting in the corner of the party room with Asia. She watched as Asia changed seats so that she could be closer to him. As soon as she sat down, they gazed deeply into one another's eyes. They then began talking and followed that up with a kiss. They continued kissing, displaying a very public display of affection, and Nancy couldn't believe what she saw. She pulled out her cell phone and quickly snapped a picture of the scene before her and then returned to her office to call James again. He didn't answer his phone, so she sent him a text message asking that he call her back right away. James replied to her immediately, letting her know he was with his girlfriend and would call her back later. That infuriated Nancy. She didn't know he had a girlfriend! She actually believed she still had a chance to get back together with him. She didn't reply back. Instead, she left the restaurant in a state of absolute fury.

Meanwhile, Dave and Asia talked about their future in between kisses. "Are you nervous about our upcoming wedding plans?" he asked. At the time, no one except the two of them and Asia's mom knew about their upcoming nuptials since their relationship was a sensitive topic due to their age difference.

As they continued to talk, Asia received a call from her dad. She gestured to Dave to be quiet. "Asia, do you know why your mom isn't answering her phone? I've tried to reach her a few times today."

"No, dad. Sorry. I don't know why, but I'll try giving her a call on three-way."

"You don't have to do that. I'll try her again later on," he replied.

"Is it important? Is everything okay?"

"No, it's not important, and yes, everything is fine." It didn't come across as truth, but he didn't want his daughter to worry. Plus, he was still under the impression that Sarah and Dave were a couple. He wasn't at all aware it was Asia and Dave, thanks to Nancy's earlier call.

After Asia hung up, she told Dave what her dad said. He didn't really care for the content of the conversation as much as he did about having to be silent when her dad called. He spoke to Asia about it, and they agreed they would no longer live in hiding. It was time for everyone to know about their relationship. Asia decided to send her dad a text, telling him that she had something very important she needed to tell him. He saw the message but didn't reply because he believed it was regarding Sarah and Dave.

****

James was obviously angry about the incoming text messages, unanswered calls to Sarah, and the call from Nancy, which had Kelly staring at him in disbelief. They were at her house having lunch when the events began to unfold, so she demanded answers as to why he allowed others to change his mood so drastically. He explained everything to her, but she knew in her heart the anger was more about Dave than Sarah or Asia. He was allowing his pride to get the best of him. "Thank you for being honest," she said as she gave him a comforting hug. James was surprised to receive a hug from Kelly. He expected her to start fussing at him, but she was calm, cool, and collected. "Everybody has something they must get over in life. Your current situation is just that," she stated. While they continued to embrace, James started smiling and told her how grateful he was to have her in his life.

James was often smiling when he was with Kelly because she was 12 years younger than him, but her level of maturity was beyond others her age. They finally released each other from their embrace when the doorbell rang. "Please have a seat. I'll be right back. It's a surprise for you," Kelly said with a big smile spread from ear to ear. James took a seat at the kitchen table and waited for her to return with the surprise.

When she returned, her father was by her side. When Kelly's dad saw James, he was startled but kept his composure. On the other hand, James thought nothing of his reaction because that was what usually happened since he was so popular in the city. Kelly introduced the men, and they shook hands. As they greeted one another, Kelly's dad told James, "You can call me Pastor Jacobs." The two had spoken on the phone on numerous occasions but had never met in person until that moment.

Pastor Jacobs took a seat at the table, and Kelly went to the refrigerator to retrieve the pitcher with her dad's favorite iced tea made of a unique blend that had been in their family for years. She then asked James if he wanted some, and he replied, "Yes, but why didn't you offer it to me before now?"

"Because I had already bought drinks with the lunch that you paid for." He smiled and nodded that he understood.

When they finished their drinks amid friendly chatter, Pastor Jacobs asked James, "Why haven't you asked to marry my daughter. After all, you've been dating for over eight months." Kelly and James were surprised that he came right out and asked that question.

"Well, Pastor Jacobs, your daughter would like for me to get a handle on my anger issues. As well, we'd like to have marriage counseling before committing to go to the next level."

Pastor Jacobs smiled and said, "Since I'm here, we can start working on your anger issues and can have your first marriage counseling session!"

During the session, Pastor Jacobs was pleased to learn the couple hadn't yet slept together. They did, however, share that they had come close to having sexual intercourse countless times. "How did you overcome those feelings?" the pastor asked.

Kelly replied, "We agreed to no nighttime visits at each other's homes and no prolonged kissing."

"Yes, but it has been hard on me because I'm not used to abstaining from sex," James added.

Pastor Jacobs then diverted the conversation to James' anger issues, which came by way of getting to the root of the problem. "You must get a grip on your anger issues before they cause you major embarrassment." James was amazed at how Pastor Jacobs helped him so easily with those few words. No one wants to be embarrassed!

The three then began to discuss marriage. Pastor Jacobs explained to the couple the ten topics of marriage counseling that he must cover, and they agreed to him proceeding. For the next three hours, they talked their way through the ten topics. Near the end of the session, Pastor Jacobs told them he wanted them to speak with one of his marriage counselors at the church to close out their marriage counseling session officially. "I believe you will be fine, as long as you address the areas that we highlighted during today's discussion. I strongly encourage both of you to consider praying and fasting in preparation for your future union. I must be honest and say I am not totally comfortable with your age difference, but I have no choice but to respect my daughter's decision." He paused for a moment before asking the next question. "James, what would you do if you found out your own daughter was in a relationship, and there was a significant age gap?"

"It would be hard to accept, but I would eventually have to accept my daughter's decision," he replied with all honesty. Pastor Jacobs smiled and shook James' hand firmly.

"One of the hardest things parents must do is let their children grow up and live with the choices they make," the pastor stated. James agreed wholeheartedly. The three of them talked for a bit longer, gently tackling James' anger issues.

Soon after, James' alarm clock sounded, reminding him not to forget about meeting his brother to go fishing. He told Kelly and Pastor Jacobs about his plans and that he had to leave immediately. He said his goodbyes and left the house to get into his SUV. As soon as he got in, he received another call from Nancy. "I'm so sorry for the interruptions, but this is very important. Please forgive me," she began.

"It's okay, Nancy. I forgive you. What's up?"

"Have you checked your text messages yet?"

"Not yet. Let me take a look. Hold on." As he scrolled through the messages from Nancy, he saw the pictures she took of Dave and Asia kissing, which sent his blood boiling.

"I just saw Dave shopping in the mall," Nancy reported.

James hung up the phone without so much as a goodbye, put the SUV in drive, and burned rubber as he sped off to the mall — as Kelly and Pastor Jacobs watched in disbelief.

****

While James was driving, he forwarded the pictures to Sarah and then called her. When she answered, he immediately began fussing at her about Asia and Dave. When he finished his rant, she sternly said, "You have the audacity to have such anger about them while simultaneously dating a 26-year-old young lady!"

"That's different. Kelly has already finished college and has her own place," he countered. Sarah disagreed, and they continued arguing, even while James drove around the mall parking lot looking for Dave's truck. Once located, he parked nearby and waited for Dave to exit the mall. A few minutes later, Dave came out and headed toward his truck. He didn't recognize James' truck, so he proceeded to open the door to his own vehicle, unaware of the danger lurking nearby. By that time, James' anger was out of control. "I see Dave. I'm going to kill him!" he said and then hung up the phone. Sarah was terrified, so she immediately called the Sheriff. James got out of his truck, walked over to Dave, and confronted him. "I know all about you and Asia!" he hollered. He kept screaming and fussing at Dave, all while getting closer and closer to him.

"Man, step back and calm down," Dave said, trying desperately to diffuse the situation.

James' fussing drew a crowd that surrounded the two, and some started recording the confrontation live on social media. James kept screaming and approaching Dave, and Dave kept recommending that he back off. Suddenly, James rushed toward Dave and swung at him, but Dave ducked and connected his fist with James' face, knocking him down to the ground. Dave then jumped on him and continuously hit him in the face. Soon, the mall police arrive and break up the fight. Shortly after, the Sheriff arrived, too.

The Sheriff knew James and Dave. He asked them, "Are y'all okay?" Neither man responded. They just stared angrily at one another. "If you do not calm down right now, I will take both of you to jail." Both remained quiet and calmed down. "Now, get into your vehicles and go straight home." The Sheriff dispersed the crowd, and everything returned to normal.

While James was driving away, his phone rang, and he answered using the Bluetooth feature in his SUV. It was Asia calling. "Dad, I understand your frustration and anger, but you have just embarrassed yourself with your actions."

"To what are you referring?" he asked.

"I'm talking about the fight between you and Dave. It's all over social media!"

James was embarrassed and apologized to his daughter. "I'm so sorry. I didn't know how to take the news of the two of you being together. I could probably have dealt with it better if Dave wasn't the one you were in a relationship with."

"I understand, and I'm sorry. I hope things will get better once you come around to accepting my decision to be with him."

"I don't know when that will happen, but I know I must do so one day. It's just too sudden of a revelation for me right now," he replied. "What about DJ?"

"DJ is Dave's son." James was in a total state of shock. Asia felt obligated to explain. "DJ's mom's last name is Jacobson. She left the city with her husband after DJ graduated. He stayed with his dad for a while but eventually moved into his own townhome. He told his dad he wanted to work for everything and not be given anything, especially knowing his dad is wealthy. DJ and I have been close friends since elementary school, but I did not meet Dave until last year. Plus, DJ has a girlfriend who is much older than he is." She paused to let all of that sink in.

"I'm so sorry. I can't apologize enough for my actions. I do not want our relationship to get any worse than what it is," James said pleadingly.

"Dad, please go home and calm down. Be safe."

"Okay. I'll call you later." While driving home, he called Kelly to apologize to her, too, since he knew she would eventually find out about the fight.

"It's okay. Can you please come over?" she asked. He agreed, and once there, the two take a long walk along the lake to help calm him down.

****

Asia called DJ to see if he had spoken to his dad since she had called him a few times, and he didn't answer. By mistake, she placed a video call, and he apparently answered without realizing it. Asia saw Tiffany in the background and was surprised but didn't say anything about it at the time. Instead, she focused on telling DJ what happened and how the incident exploded on social media. DJ was instantly alarmed. He checked his phone for missed called but didn't have any. "I do have a text message from my dad telling me he was going for a swim to cool off and would call me when he finished," he reported. "He also asked me to let you know that he was okay," DJ continued. Asia was relieved. After he finished reading the message, Asia smiled and told him she saw Tiffany and knew who the mystery woman was. "Mind your own business," DJ said with a smile before disconnecting the call.

Asia was smiling when she sent Dave a text, asking him to call her when he finished swimming.

Tiffany was staring at DJ in horror when he turned around and walked back to the couch where she was seated. "I believe Asia saw me when you were on that video call," she said sadly.

"She did, but it's okay," DJ replied while embracing her in a hug.

She pulled back and looked at him in disbelief, alarmed that he would say such a thing. "What makes you so certain she will not tell the world about us?" DJ then told her about Asia and his dad's relationship. Tiffany was blown away, and even moreso after DJ showed her the social media recording of the two men fighting that Asia told him about. She was not at all surprised by James' actions, but she started to laugh when she saw him get knocked to the ground.

After watching the video, DJ told her he was tired of hiding their relationship. Tiffany paused and then told him, "Sophia already knows about us, too." She also told him about Travis and how they sought marriage counseling with Pastor Jacobs to see where their hearts really were. During the session, Travis revealed he still didn't want to be married and only sought to please his daughter. Tiffany also revealed she was not in love with Travis either and that she was only considering getting back with him just to appease her daughter, too. In the end, they agreed just to be friends. They haven't even spoken since the counseling session, but they made sure to explain everything to Sophia. Thankfully, Sophia understood and was happy to know her parents were at least still friends.

DJ was startled by the revelation and understood she was doing the right thing, but he was even more pleased knowing he didn't have to compete with Travis for her. "I have a confession," he said, which immediately gained Tiffany's attention. "My dad knows about our relationship, too." Both of them burst out laughing.

Tiffany called Sophia on video. When she answered, she saw DJ in the background waving at her. She laughed and then said to him, "My mom must have just told you that I already know." DJ replied with a thumbs-up. Tiffany then suggested they all should have dinner together soon. Sophia agreed and told her mom she would call her the next day to set it up. After they hung up, Tiffany turned and noticed DJ staring at her. "Why are you looking at me like that?"

"Because I am so in love with you and hope we are together forever," he replied. Tiffany was stunned by his remark but not overly surprised. Both had expressed a deep affection for one another in the past, but for him to say it aloud at that moment caught her off guard. She leaned over, pulled him close, and kissed him passionately. When they stopped for a breather, DJ asked, "What would it take for you to say yes to a marriage proposal from me?"

"You don't have to do anything extra. Just ask when you believe you are ready."

"Great! I will definitely ask in the near future, especially after opening my own business and buying a house. I need to be sure I am financially stable and able to provide a home for my bride-to-be."

Tiffany smiled and told him, "I am so proud of you and glad we had that discussion before you told me about your upcoming goals."

"I need to go and check on my dad. I'll call you later," DJ said as he walked to the door with Tiffany by his side. They embrace one more time before he leaves.

****

After DJ departed, Tiffany called Chelsea to tell her the news about Dave, as well as the update on her and DJ. Chelsea was surprised about the fight but not about both relationships. "I already knew about Asia and Dave. I'll explain how I knew at a later date. As for you, Tiffany, congratulations on your relationship with DJ—the one you managed to hide from practically everyone! I have my own update. Nick and I are in the lobby outside of Pastor Williams' office. We decided to skip the traditional wedding and arranged for an immediate exchange of vows after being counseled by Pastor Williams. Since his schedule was free, he agreed to do our short notice wedding very soon. He even said he had another short-notice wedding story he wanted to share with us at another time. I have to run now, though. We'll catch up very soon!" Chelsea hung up the phone and focused her attention on the task at hand.

Nick and Chelsea told Pastor Williams they only wanted a maximum of 20 people at their wedding. The pastor suggested they use one of the conference rooms in the church that was set up for small, intimate weddings. They agreed and started discussing other particulars regarding the service. When they were finished with their meeting with Pastor Williams, they left the church and immediately started calling the few people they chose to be in attendance on their special day.

The last person Chelsea called was Asia. Although she was sure Sarah would tell her, Chelsea wanted to call everyone personally. When Asia answered the phone, Chelsea told her the fabulous news. Asia was delighted and then told her about her relationship with Dave. Chelsea was surprised and excited at the same time.

After their call, Asia continued with her own wedding planning with Dave, which was in stark contrast to Chelsea and Nick's plans. They were planning a traditional wedding with many guests. Amid their chatter, Dave stopped and apologized to Asia for the fight he had with her dad. "I promise never to fight him again," he said with seriousness. Asia smiled and then hugged him because she knew he was sincere. Shortly after the bulk of their plans were set, the two of them began informing everyone about their wedding and told them more details are forthcoming.

She's Ready at 18... He's Ready at 38!

Chapter Six: Dealing With It

With a new month came so much new excitement. The ladies decided to have another outing, but with their daughters included. Chelsea asked if the evening could be doubled as a bachelorette party for her since her wedding was less than a week away. None of the women objected to her proposal as all looked forward to getting together again.

Friday night seemed to come fast. All week long leading up to their outing, each lady was excited about coming together to talk about the changes in their life. They arrived at Top Shelf at their regular time with their daughters, got out of their cars, greeted one another, and then Sarah said a prayer that included a special prayer for the new relationships and Sophia's pregnancy.

After she prayed and the group started walking toward the lounge, a customized van pulled up with the lounge's name on its side. Two men got out and told the ladies that the owner sent the van to pick them up. Tiffany recognized the men as friends of DJ. "How did both of you get jobs here?" she asked.

"We know the owner," one of them replied. The ladies thought nothing more of it because Ricky had the paperwork to buy the lounge and was always helping people. Lizzie, on the other hand, looked puzzled by their simple response. She thought it was a tactic drummed up by Ricky to try and ease his way back into her life. Tiffany thanked the gentlemen, and they all climbed aboard.

The driver took the ladies to the back of the lounge to the vehicle elevator that is typically reserved exclusively for management and VIPs, which thoroughly excited all of them. When they arrived on the second level, four additional men awaited their exit from the van. Each lady was given a dozen roses, but Chelsea was given two dozen, plus balloons. They were then escorted into the lounge, where they were treated like celebrities, with a multitude of photographers taking pictures of them. The ladies were overjoyed at the superb treatment they received. They were then led to a VIP section they had never been to before that was roped off and decorated with balloons and various other decorations. The women were regulars at Top Shelf for years and had never seen that type of display for anyone else—including celebrities—so that made them all feel extra special.

As they took their seats, the waiter approached and told them, "Via compliments of the new owner, all of your drinks are free all night. He will be joining you shortly." A few minutes later, DJ walked into their VIP section. All of them wondered why DJ was there, especially Tiffany.

DJ was smiling broadly while they stared at him in silence. "Ladies, I am the new owner!" They were in disbelief because everyone knew he was recently working as a manager at a different restaurant. He explained, "Nick had previously agreed to sell the lounge to Ricky, but after Lizzie broke his heart, he wanted to move out of the city, so he canceled the purchase. Ricky had already reached out to me about becoming one of the managers here, which was how I knew the deal fell apart. Once I saw an opportunity to purchase the lounge, I asked my father for a loan. Once he received the money, he used it to buy Top Shelf from Nick." Tiffany was surprised because DJ never told her about the purchase. He had purposely kept it a secret, as he wanted to surprise her. Everyone at the table was shocked and even moreso when DJ said, "I also came over here to speak briefly with my woman." The women looked around for the lady he referred to until Tiffany stood and reached out her hand for DJ to lead her away from the table.

As the group remained in a silent state of shock, Asia and Sophia smiled because they were already aware of that budding relationship. Tiffany turned for just a moment to toss them a smile before disappearing into the crowd. They were so happy for her, knowing she was a loving person who deserved someone who would take great care of her heart. They continued talking about how happy they were for Tiffany, and shortly after, she returned to the table. They were surprised because they thought she would spend more time with DJ. "That was his way of letting everyone know we are a couple," she explained. "We are no longer hiding our relationship."

As they were talking, their significant others entered the lounge on the first floor. When the disc jockey acknowledged them, everyone—including the ladies—focused all their attention on them. They were astonished at the sight before them, as the guys never came together. DJ, however, had prearranged the outing for the guys and sat them in the lounge's lower-level VIP section so that the ladies could enjoy themselves on the upper level.

After the guys walked by, Asia said, "I wonder if my dad is going to show up."

Sarah replied, "Probably not. He's likely still embarrassed about that viral social media post."

Asia then asked to be excused. She needed to call and check on her father, so she walked to one of the corners of the lounge and placed the call. He picked up immediately, surprised and excited that she called him. "I'm just calling to check on you. I love you, dad."

He was honored that she thought enough to check on him and replied, "Thank you, sweetie. I'm okay. I love you, too." As they continued their conversation, he noticed the background noise. "Where are you?" She told him about the outing, and he said he was happy she was spending quality time with the ladies. "I'm with Kelly right now at her house, relaxing and watching movies," he reported. Kelly knew Asia was on the phone, so they spoke briefly, exchanging greetings.

Once her dad got back on the phone, Asia said, "I gotta go now to get back to the group. Continue enjoying your time with Kelly. We'll talk again soon." They said their goodbyes, and both returned to their previous engagements.

Asia returned to the table to find the ladies bubbling over in laughter. "What did I miss? Why are you laughing so hard?"

Her mother responded, "Us mothers are the ones who keep telling our daughters to leave them young boys alone but look at us now!" They roared with laughter again. The women didn't want their daughters dating older guys, yet somehow, their influence helped create the current relationships.

Smiling, Asia said, "I'm thankful to have Dave. I believe age can be overrated if one's mind isn't right." The women smiled, agreed, and complimented her for such a mature response.

****

A few hours later, Sarah texted Jason to see if the guys were ready to leave. After confirming with the other men that they were ready, they agreed to meet the ladies at the bar to escort them out of the lounge. All of them were excited because that was the first time they got together as couples, and it was very special to them. They met at the bar and walked out together, but Tiffany stayed behind with DJ.

Chelsea told them she needed everyone to be at the church earlier than expected as the couples made their way to their cars. "We had to move the start time up an hour earlier because we are catching a flight for our honeymoon." Everyone agreed to arrive early, got into their respective cars, and departed the parking garage to head home.

The following day, Jason showed up at Sarah's house three hours early to take her to the wedding as requested by Chelsea. When Sarah opened the door, Jason handed her a dozen mixed roses. She was surprised and gave him a joyful hug. "It's been years since I received roses from a man. I truly appreciate you being the one who broke the drought of me not receiving them." Without another word, Jason got down on one knee. Sarah was immediately filled with fear because she hoped he was not about to propose to her. If so, she was prepared to tell him no. However, when she looked down, she noticed he was tying the laces on his dress shoes.

When he looked back up at her, he could see she was slightly bothered. He smiled at her because he immediately knew she was expecting him to propose. "Relax, Sarah. I learned from my dad to do that just to gauge your interest. If you were smiling when I looked at you, then I knew you were prepared to say yes to a proposal. Conversely, if you looked bothered, I knew not to even think about asking for your hand in marriage at that time." Sarah was amazed at the story's simplicity, but he had to confess he was just joking.

While they were laughing, Asia came downstairs, prepared to ride with them to the wedding. Her mom told her about what Jason had done, and they all laughed about it. Eventually, they are ready to go and get into Jason's truck. He had to be there even earlier than the other guests because he had the honor of being the Best Man.

When they arrived at the church, they noticed Nick was already parked in the parking lot, but they noticed Chelsea was not with him when they parked next to him. He explained that she had already gone inside 20 minutes earlier with her mother and sisters. Sarah—Chelsea's Maid of Honor—and Asia quickly hugged Jason at the same time and then hurried into the building to find the bride-to-be.

Jason and Nick eventually walked into the church where Pastor Williams was waiting for them. The pastor pulled Nick aside and escorted him into the office. "You and I need to have one final talk," he told Nick. "I've already spoken with Chelsea about ten minutes ago."

Roughly two hours later, someone announced over the PA system that the wedding would commence in 15 minutes. Chelsea looked as beautiful as ever as her dad escorted her into the conference room when the ceremony began. Nick started crying as he watched his bride approaching. It was a beautiful moment, and then Pastor Williams performed the ceremony. After they said their "I dos," everyone has happy for them as they walked through the venue waving at the guests. The newlyweds took pictures, followed by a short reception because they were leaving soon on a private jet to Dubai for their honeymoon — a gift from one of Nick's friends.

While the bride and groom were making their last rounds to greet the guests, Asia received a call from her dad asking if she wanted to have a late lunch with him. "I'm sorry, dad. I can't. I'm at a wedding right now."

"Please tell me it's not your wedding! And you didn't invite me?!" he joked.

She laughed and told him, "No! It's Chelsea and Nick's wedding!"

"That's okay. It would've been a quick lunch anyway because I have an appointment with Pastor Jacobs this afternoon. We'll do it another day. Goodbye for now. I love you," James said.

"I love you, too, dad. Goodbye." Asia returned to the wedding festivities, and James grabbed a bite to eat before meeting with Pastor Jacobs.

She's Ready at 18... He's Ready at 38!

****

James arrived early for his meeting with Pastor Jacobs. Before their meeting, Pastor Jacobs asked James to go for a walk with him throughout the church. Other than the presence of the normal deacons, the pastor and James were the only other ones there. As they walked, they talked about God and family. Pastor Jacobs then turned their attention to the topic of their meeting. James was surprised because he expected the discussion to be held in the privacy of the pastor's office.

"Whenever the opportunity arises, I like to walk either inside the church on the church grounds to do my sessions," Pastor Jacobs explained. "It's like being on neutral ground. Some counselees love the strategy because they feel open and not closed in like normal counseling sessions. Please use your cell phone to take notes."

The session was focused on James' attitude. As they walked and talked, James became more relaxed when it became apparent that Pastor Jacobs grasped the root of his anger issues, which dated back to the verbal and mental abuse he received from his father. Pastor Jacobs gave James a few suggestions to help him overcome during moments of anger, which James noted in his phone. Significant progress was made during the session, and the pastor was impressed with what he learned about James at that time. The session benefitted Pastor Jacobs, too, because although he is a clergyman, he's also a concerned father—especially since James was dating his daughter. When the session came to an end, James agreed to monthly follow-ups.

As James exited the church, Kelly was outside waiting for him. She hugged her dad and, while they embraced, the pastor kept one arm around her and then turned around to face James. "When are you going to marry my daughter?"

"As soon as your daughter says yes," James responded while gazing into Kelly's eyes.

She smiled and said, "As soon as the counseling sessions are over and my father is pleased, then I'll be ready to marry James." Pastor Jacobs was so proud of her and hugged her tightly. James smiled and embraced Pastor Jacobs before saying goodbye so that he and Kelly could leave to get an early dinner.

"I always feel my best when you are with me," James told her.

"You must learn how to channel that same energy when you're not with me," she commented.

"Maybe you're right. Have you ever considered becoming a counselor?" Kelly laughed at his question and told him she had been asked that on numerous occasions. As they walked to their vehicles, continuing to laugh and enjoy themselves, Pastor Jacobs watched their interaction, which warmed his heart immensely to see both of them so happy together.

Chapter Seven: Wedding Week

A few weeks after Nick and Chelsea's wedding, Dave and Asia prepared for the upcoming nuptials that were set to take place in one week. As the couple sat on the deck of Dave's house, relaxing and discussing their future, Asia said, "I want to finish college and open my financial consulting business."

"You know you have my full support. I have no doubt you will be successful," he encouraged, especially knowing that her passion stemmed from watching her mother be involved in many business ventures. Dave was pleased because business was something the two of them had in common. He was, after all, a millionaire. Most people did not know that about him, and Asia didn't learn about his millionaire status until recently. After discussing business, they turned the focus to their wedding.

As they go over their guest list, Asia sent a text to the wedding planner to get a current count of the guests who confirmed. She received a rapid response that stated the only person who had not RSVP'd was her dad. She made sure he received an invitation and knew he received it because it was delivered by certified mail with a signature required. She did not want to give it in person, knowing he didn't support her decision to marry Dave. Each time she spoke to her dad about it, he would get very angry. Asia understood why but refused to let it bother her.

Later in the day, Dave prepared to take Asia home. Although she had spent the night on many occasions, they agreed she wouldn't stay over until after they were married as it got closer to their wedding day. Both insisted on doing the right things. "I sure will be glad when we can spend every day and night together," Asia stated with a sigh. Their initial meeting happened a few days before her 19th birthday, and they'd been dating for ten months before marriage became their focus, with her 20th birthday just over the horizon.

When he dropped off Asia, he noticed Jason leaving her mom's house. Once out of the car, she stopped to hug Jason and give him a high-five. Jason then walked over to Dave's truck, where the two men talked for a few minutes. Sarah came and stood beside Asia as both looked out the window at the men talking. Asia pinched her mom and smiled before walking into the living room to discuss the upcoming wedding.

****

Bachelor and Bachelorette Parties

With just a few more days left before the wedding, Dave and Asia were excited beyond measure. They were finally in a happy place with no more hiding and no worries. After living many months in secret, they were almost entirely free to be themselves.

While having a meeting to discuss the final additions to the wedding, Dave received a call from his son, DJ. "Dad, I know it's short notice, but there's a bachelor party planned for you tomorrow night."

"I'm not really interested, son, but I'll think about it. Right now, we're finalizing our wedding arrangements. I'll call you back later."

"What is it that you're not really interested in doing?" Asia asked when he hung up from the call.

"DJ mentioned there's a bachelor party planned for me tomorrow night."

With a smile on her face, she confessed that she was the one who planned the party for him and that she really wanted him to go. Dave explained that he felt uncomfortable because he knew how rowdy those parties could get. "Why do you want me to have a bachelor party?"

"Although you've been to a few, I want you to experience one for yourself. Plus, I can promise this party won't be raunchy." After talking about it for a few more minutes, he agreed to go to the party — even with short notice. "I'm glad you agreed when you did because we only had one more hour to cancel the reservation or lose our money!"

The next day came, and Dave was excited about his upcoming party. DJ drove him there, and when they entered the room, Dave immediately noticed the massive cake in the center surrounded by big gifts. One of the guys said, "We know you like to do everything big, which is the theme of this party!" The cake itself was the size of a circular dinner tabletop. Although the gift packages were oversized, the actual gifts were normal-sized. For entertainment, there were comedians and a few celebrity singers. Nick was connected to many entertainers, which is how the celebrities were present.

Everything was going great until one of the security guards called DJ on his cell. He reported to DJ that James was at the main entrance asking to speak to Dave. DJ relays the message, and both men leave the party to go and see what James wanted to talk about. They didn't tell anyone else where they were going because they didn't want things to get out of hand again, especially considering most of the men at the party didn't like James. As they approached the entrance, they noticed James was by himself chatting it up with the guards. "Everything will be alright, son. Go back upstairs. Let James and I talk. The guards will be right here." Dave instructed DJ to do that because he knew how overprotective his son could be.

Once DJ was out of sight, Dave walked forward and motioned for the guards to step away. When they did, Dave and James engaged in conversation. Meanwhile, DJ was peeking around the corner to ensure he was okay. When DJ saw James reach out his hand to shake his dad's hand, he quickly grabbed his phone and took a few pictures of them actually shaking hands. He was amazed that the two men did so after over 18 years of ill feelings between them and continued to watch their interaction carefully.

James was the first to speak regarding why he was there. "I just wanted to let you know I am still trying to cope with the relationship you have with my daughter. It's hard, man. Really hard. But I don't want any trouble. I needed to come to see you and apologize for my previous actions."

"We both need to do better," Dave replied. Although James apologized, he didn't look like he was sincere. He turned to walk away but saluted Dave before getting in his SUV to leave.

DJ couldn't believe it — and he would not have believed it if he hadn't seen it happen with his own eyes. As Dave approached the elevator to head back to the party, DJ came from around the corner smiling and hugged his dad. As quiet as it was kept, DJ was extremely happy to see his dad practice what he preached about doing better to maintain peace.

Once back in the party room, all of the guys wanted to know where Dave and DJ went. Dave told them about James' visit to try and ease the tension between them. That report pleased the partygoers, so they returned to enjoying themselves. As everyone enjoyed the entertainment, DJ sent Asia a picture of Dave and James shaking hands.

****

When Asia received the picture, she cried tears of joy. She texted DJ back, thanking him, and then returned to enjoying her bachelorette party. The ladies had planned Asia's party to be held at the same time as the bachelor party since she had shared with them how she planned Dave's party. Dave played a huge part in the planning. Asia was so happy to know Dave was actively engaged in creating happiness for her.

Dave texted Asia to let her know her dad came by the party to apologize. She didn't tell him that DJ had already sent a picture, but she did tell him she was so happy about them being calm in each other's presence for a change. Eventually, she told the ladies at her party about the exchange between the two men.

All of them were amazed except for Sarah. She had previously witnessed James do something similar, only to return to his unstable ways. She then paused that thought and told herself that maybe he had changed since then. Sarah walked over and hugged Asia, telling her the wedding was going to be awesome!

When the party was over, the women escorted Asia out of the room to the waiting limousine that would take her to a helicopter. The helicopter then flew her to a rooftop where Dave was waiting for her for a late-night romantic talk over tea. After being escorted to the table by a waitstaff member, she and Dave embraced in a warm hug. "How did you know when the party would be over?" she asked.

"I didn't know but took a chance on the timing. I'm glad it all worked out! The way this night worked out demonstrates how wonderful our lives will be and so much more," he stated confidently. They talked and enjoyed the night. When it was time to part ways, they gave each other a passionate kiss before the helicopter took her back to the limousine, which drove her back to her mother's house.

****

Meanwhile, James was already at Sarah's house because he wanted to see Asia when she returned from her bachelorette party. He didn't believe he was going to attend the wedding and wanted to see her one more time before then.

As the limousine approached her mom's house, Asia saw Kelly's car parked outside. James got out of the passenger's side holding flowers and a gift for his daughter. When she exited the limo, she ran over to her father, and they embraced like they hadn't seen one another in years.

Kelly was delighted to witness how happy James was when with his daughter. She was also so proud of him for making such great progress with his anger issues. At that very moment, she made up in her mind to never leave him because she knew he was a good man and believed he would soon overcome all of his major issues.

As father and daughter embrace, Asia says, "I am so proud of you and the way you handled yourself with Dave at the bachelor party."

"Wait. How did you know about that?" he inquired.

"Dave told me, of course!" James smiled because he expected Dave to tell her.

They embrace again, and he said to her, "I believe I'm much better than I used to be and will continue pressing forward to be a better man overall." They talked for a bit longer before he said, "I'm going to go now so that you can get some rest before your big day tomorrow."

Asia gave him one last hug, turned to wave at Kelly, and went into the house, waving at her dad and Kelly before closing the door.

****

She's Ready at 18... He's Ready at 38!

When James got back into the car, Kelly hugged him tightly. They kissed and continued to embrace until James saw a truck pulling up. It was Jason. He waved at James and Kelly as he drove by and parked in front of Sarah's house. Kelly felt the situation would turn sour if they stayed parked, so she started the car and drove off. James looked in the side mirror as they drove away and saw Sarah come out of the house. He continued watching and saw Sarah and Jason engage in a kiss. Instantly, he became enraged but didn't let Kelly see his anger.

"I'm glad Sarah and Asia are happy," he managed to say. Kelly smiled because she believed he was sincere. She then grabbed his hand to ensure he focused on her, not Sarah. He looked over at her and said, "Stop the car." When she pulled over the side of the road, he removed his seatbelt, reached over, and hugged her. He was crying when he told her, "I am thankful to God for blessing me with you. For a while, I started to believe I was a loser because everything I tried to enjoy was always taken away from me, or I lost it."

"No, honey. You are definitely not a loser. You are a winner! I am the one who's blessed to have such an awesome man in my life." James smiled, and they kissed again before Kelly got back on the road and dropped James off at home.

When they arrived at James' house, Kelly asked, "Are you going to the wedding?"

"No. I don't want to go because honestly, I do not believe my anger is completely under control yet."

She respected his honesty and did not press for him to attend. Both then got out of the car and hugged one more time before he turned to go inside. He then stopped midstride and pleaded with Kelly to spend the night with him since it was late, and he did not want her driving alone to the other side of town. She agreed, and they entered his house together.

Wedding Day

Asia and Dave's wedding day arrived. While everyone was getting prepared for the ceremony, Asia stepped aside to call her dad to see if he had a change of heart. When he answered, he listened to her plea but responded, "I'm sorry. I thought about it all night. I simply cannot support you marrying Dave." That response brought on a flood of tears.

When Sarah saw her daughter crying, she ran over and snatched the phone from Asia's hand. "Who is this?!"

"It's me, Sarah," James replied. Sarah walked outside to speak to him. Once outside the church, she fussed and cussed him out. She also belittled him by saying he was a sorry excuse for a man, which only proved to make him angrier. He hung up the phone on her, blacked out, and punched a nearby wall before realizing he wasn't at home—he was at a local convenience store he had stopped by to get a few items on his way home.

The store owner knew James and asked, "What's wrong, man?" When James shared with the man why he was angry, the store owner agreed with him and said, "I get it. I probably would've shot Dave if I were you."

The store owner's words rang through James' ears like he was challenging the angry father. It didn't help at all that James still harbored ill feelings because he believed Dave not only stole his daughter, but he also ruined his football career. The owner kept talking about 'what he would do,' which served to raise Dave's level of anger to its highest level. As James stormed out of the store, the owner asked where he was going. "I'm going to blow off some steam!" James growled. The man knew James was a concealed weapon carrier, and he felt terrible about potentially stirring up thoughts of James actually shooting Dave.

On the way out the door, some friends of Dave were walking into the store. They taunted him about the fight they saw on social media. By then, his blood was white-hot boiling. He didn't say a word to the group, but that didn't stop their teasing. As James got into his SUV, one of Dave's friends yelled out, "And he got your daughter!" James peeled out of there, determined to really hurt Dave. He had never been that angry in his life and set his sights on driving to the wedding to seriously cause Dave bodily harm.

****

Back at the church, the ladies worked diligently to cheer up Asia. It didn't take long, and once she refocused on her special day, she was extremely happy and vowed not to allow anything more to disrupt her future. Simultaneously, the men just completed a prayer session led by Jason. They were all excited for Dave because they believed he was an awesome person who deserved nothing but the best — and they were also grateful for being chosen to play a crucial part in his day. With all of his high-profile friends, he could have easily selected any of them over the group that stood with him.

Just as the wedding was about to start, it was interrupted by Asia's dad. While the guests were seated in the sanctuary, he walked through and headed straight for where Dave and his friends were waiting to enter. He glared at Pastor Williams with anger but kept on moving to locate Dave. When James made it to the room where Dave and the other guys were, he turned the knob on the door, noticed it was locked, and then kicked it open. James pulled out his gun, aimed it squarely at Dave, and yelled for the other men to get out. As soon as they exited, James said, "I'm not going to shoot you. I want to fight you man-to-man once and for all to end it." He placed the gun on the table, swung at Dave with a closed fist, and missed. He then grabbed Dave and wrestled him to the floor, at which time James started swinging wildly at Dave but could not connect with a good punch.

Word got back to Asia that her father was in the building with a gun pointed at Dave. She ran to the room, but the guys wouldn't let her get through. She left and ran around to another entrance that was unlocked. When she finally entered the room, Dave made eye contact with her. James took advantage of the moment with that brief distraction and landed a series of punches to Dave's face. Dave, however, remembered his promise to Asia not to fight her dad ever again, so he didn't fight back.

Asia knew Dave wasn't going to fight back, so she begged her dad to stop. He didn't listen. He just kept punching and punching Dave until he blacked out from being hit numerous times—and he kept punching even after it was apparent Dave was completely out of it. Asia saw that her father was about to possibly kill Dave. She panicked, saw the gun James left on the table, grabbed it, and shot James.

When the police finally arrive, they immediately arrest Asia, place her in a police car, and take her to the station. The EMTs arrive shortly after. James and his gunshot wound and Dave with his serious facial injuries are rushed to the same hospital emergency room in separate ambulances.

****

Later that day, Pastor Jacobs visited James in the hospital and spoke to him about forgiveness. After talking for a few minutes, the pastor said a prayer and then asked James if he, too, would like to pray. "Yes, pastor, I would. Thank you."

During his prayer, James asked the Lord to forgive him and then rededicated his life to Christ.

When the men finished praying, James noticed Asia, Sarah, and Kelly standing in the doorway. The ladies heard the prayers and were all overjoyed. James, however, was shocked to see them and then asked for their forgiveness. All three of them stated in their own way simultaneously that they forgave him. "I'm so sorry I crashed your wedding and stopped you from getting married, Asia," he said.

Pastor Jacobs found that the perfect time to share with James an event from the past. "Asia and Dave were married on her 18th birthday—the day you couldn't make it home. They had a private wedding that I officiated, with Sarah and DJ in attendance as their witnesses. No one else knew about the wedding. Since you missed them exchanging their vows on that day and they believed you wouldn't take it well had you known, they agreed to have a public ceremony and invite everyone."

James was shocked and saddened, but he was no longer upset. He felt bad that his issues had such a negative impact on all of them. Shortly afterward, Jason wheeled Dave into the room in a wheelchair. No one expected Dave to enter, but Jason wheeled him over to James' bedside. The tension in the air could have been cut with a knife.

James asked Dave for forgiveness, and Dave forgave him. The men spoke a few more kind words to each other and then simultaneously reached out to shake each other's hand then embrace in a brotherly hug. Both shed tears, which caused Asia to start crying, too.

Pastor Jacobs said it best for all when he shouted, "Thank You, Lord!

Nuggets for the Readers

Essentially, every situation regarding age differences in marriages stands on its own merit. In some cultures, age is just a number, while in others, it is a legal measuring stick. In other cultures, when particular monetary conditions are met (both parties do not need money to prosper), the age difference seems to be nonexistent. There are numerous factors to consider when referencing age differences in marriage, for no single factor is applicable for all situations. If it is a legal age difference in the union without deception or darkness, I believe that it should be respected, just as "normal" marriages are respected. I do, however, acknowledge that not everyone is going to respect marriages with a significant age difference — but I believe we must at least try.

For the Singles

Being single can be a struggle if you desire to be married, and marriage has yet to manifest. It worsens when all your friends are married or almost every potential mate you meet "fits the bill" but is unavailable because they are already married. Sometimes, it is the timing. Sometimes, it is the environment. Sometimes, the individual is not ready. Sometimes, it is the individual's taste. Sometimes, it is the company the individual keeps that influences bad selections. Other times, the right one simply has not shown up.

There are other reasons why being single can be frustrating but know that being single is not a bad thing. It's only what the individuals make it to be. The individual must not allow outside influences to rush them out of the single life. Many love being single because they know what is best for them, and everyone else must respect that person's decision.

In being single, please do not place yourself on someone's bench waiting to get into the starting lineup. That is a mistake many singles make. They find themselves settling for a piece of someone — anyone — to help them massage a piece of themselves, but that should not be happening if the other person is already in a relationship. Why? Because having just a piece of a person should not disrupt peace in their household or your own.

If being single makes you happy, then enjoy it. Try not to envy those who are married. Keep in mind "everything that glitters isn't gold." Don't pressure yourself to get married but do pray about it and protect yourself from those who are seeking individuals who desire a relationship or marriage.

Remember this: Just because they see you as a rare jewel and they want you in their pool does not mean you have to swim with them!

For the Married: Praying and Fasting

A great initiative within a marriage is praying and fasting together. Praying and fasting help to curve the dependency of the flesh while elevating a spirit-filled union. Some marriage counselors promote praying and fasting before marriage because they are ways to usher in the assistance needed to confirm the pending union. During the effort, both parties must ask the Lord to help them in their decision by asking Him to confirm their relationship. In many instances, relationships are severed, while others are confirmed based on what is revealed through praying and fasting. This mostly works when both the requestors are Christians with clean hands and pure hearts.

Additionally, praying and fasting is a must in marriage because it will help heal, bind, loose, and protect as needed. The

Holy Spirit will also help reveal hidden things within the marriage and expose spiritual efforts formed against the union.

Please make it a practice to pray and fast before and during the marriage, as they are tools you can use for a lifetime.

Wisdom Nuggets

Our hope is for couples who are considering marriage and those already married to please keep the Lord in your union via the Holy Spirit. The Holy Spirit will help you daily by being the water to your tree (your marriage). Both of us were married previously and experienced marriages without both parties leaning on the Holy Spirit.

Remember that your intentions to get married are fuel, so please make sure your intentions are good. Communicate and encourage one another daily. Although every day is not perfect, please tell your spouse that you love them every day and provide them good compliments on how they look. Please do not let the sun go down on your wrath. Please do not try to rush agreements or answers to issues unless it is an emergency. Please do not assume your mate knows what you are thinking, and do not assume you know what your mate is thinking. Be willing to make the same sacrifices. Remember that both of you bring the value needed for your marriage to be priceless.

There is so much more we could say, but we simply want to encourage all marriages to be the example of marriage.

Blessings!

~ **Calvin and Kenya Brown** ~

Words of wisdom for marriages:

Keep God at the center. Be considerate of, flexible with, and understanding of each other. Serve the Lord together with your time, abilities, and money. Learn what the other values or would be a meaningful way to show them love. Have prayer time together. Fight fair by staying on topic and avoiding personal attacks. Do not let the sun go down on your anger by sincerely apologizing as often as necessary. Live modestly. Invest or save any increase (i.e., bonus or raise). Keep the proper order of God->Spouse->Children. Have long-term Christian couples in your lives that you can get advice from about marriage and parenting. Make a dated, running list of blessings and things you are thankful for that will fill multiple volumes of notebooks (include prayers, goals, and dreams). Doing those things have worked for us since we married in 1993.

May God bless your marriage!
~ Ryan and Jennifer Mann ~

She's Ready at 18… He's Ready at 38!

Warren Griffin:

I believe the most quintessential part of any relationship is communication. When everything breaks down, the only remedies for fixing problems are communicating and working through them. With trust rounding in second, communication is of the utmost importance. A long-term marriage needs communication and trust to survive because when all else fails, those two pillars are essential for the couple to stand on. In my opinion, everything a marriage needs falls under those two principles. Sex, money, and material things will be a rollercoaster throughout a long-term marriage or relationship. Although essential, they cannot fix anything when the relationship has gone south. With communication and trust, be ready for a healthy relationship or marriage.

Kimberly Griffin:

Being in a relationship requires dedication. You must be willing to dedicate your time and your love. You must also be willing to share everything that is around you. In my opinion, relationships come in several steps. You must follow them to be at least 80% authentic with your significant other within all of them. No ties will be 100% all the time. Relationships take work to maintain. Even if you are in one for 20 years, there will often be disagreements. Each person within the relationship will have their strengths and weaknesses on a particular subject or certain things that pertain to life. You must work together to learn from each other and later share with those who may be just getting started. You can teach them how to mend the relationship and the things they should avoid. The essential thing in any relationship is to have God in your life. Without Him, the connection may not be as secure and tight as you want it to be because the enemy will filter his way in.

~ **Warren and Kimberly Griffin** ~

She's Ready at 18... He's Ready at 38!

For Diane and me, once the "I Do's" were stated, the real work began. We have been married for 22 years now, but marriage is not easy. We laugh more than we fight, but it still takes true dedication to make it work for this long. I'm not being negative or pessimistic; I'm being honest. Marriage (or any other type of relationship) is about more than just sex and romance. We believe trust is more important than anything — even more important than love. Why? You can love someone because of a strong sense of concern or wellbeing for them. However, if you can't trust the person, your relationship will fail. The lack of trust will cause an unmanageable amount of emotional stress to the other partner. It's just not fair when only one partner is trustworthy, and the other is not.

Another aspect that has kept us together throughout the years is a good sense of communication. We work out our issues (even if we are yelling) to communicate our true feelings. Diane and I feel if we keep secrets or strong feelings to ourselves, we will eventually erode the trust we have in each other. We can tell each other anything, and that is an incredible feeling!

~ **Greg and Diane Blanche** ~

Relationship Quotes

They say, "Happy wife, happy life," but also remember, "Happy hubby gets a little chubby"!

Those who tame their appetite will focus on one meal and also avoid more than food poison!

They who close the door to the cookies have also made themselves vegans!

If they don't like your spouse, they shouldn't be allowed in your house!

It is not okay to communicate with people of the opposite sex and forbid your spouse to do the same!

Forgive them, do not parole them!

Your body is not for recreational use!

Marry to get into something, not out of something!

Giving too many benefits of the doubt could have you wasting time and truly missing out!

Just like you shouldn't rely on a cover to judge a book or believe everyone in the kitchen can cook, highlights that if you ignore the contents, you could be wasting precious time spent!

Life is too short to be taking the long road to peace!

Most of the people attracted to you want a piece of you while not having a single care about the peace within you!

Sleep in your bed, not on your responsibilities!

Iron out the wrinkles now so that you won't have to press them during the marriage!

It's best to have a counterweight than an anchor if the anchor is not a good thing!

Lowering your standards to raise your average could also have you striking out!

The silent treatment can invite outside noise that can silence your relationship!

Anger will keep you stuck in places you don't need to be while also keeping you from places you should be!

Secondhand smoke kills relationships, so please stop inhaling bad relationship advice!

You might be the total package at the wrong address!

Whatever you are doing outside the presence of your spouse, you are still in the presence of God!

You should rather sleep naked on cold concrete than in a hot nightmare!

The grass might look greener on the other side, but please remember that new grass comes with dirt, too!

You might fit the description, but you're not the prescription!

If you read it right when you receive it, the faster you could send it back to the sender instead of staying stuck!

You should rather the Lord deliver you a timely measure than to go forth in your own way and measure!

She's Ready at 18... He's Ready at 38!

Are You Thinking About Marriage?

It is not like Nike (Just Do It™), nor is it like Burger King (Have It Your Way™). If it is like Capital One (What's in Your Wallet?™) and centered on the flesh, then it has no true foundation, and that's how it will end. If its foundation is Christ, then it is unbreakable! Take your relationship to God like Reebok (I Am What I Am™). Then, it will be like Allstate (You're in Good Hands™). When you know that God has joined you and your mate, both of you will always be like McDonald's (I'm Loving It™)!

Three Phases of Life

What are your thoughts concerning talking about marriage on the first date? Many individuals do not want to discuss marriage early on because they believe it will chase the other person away. Others believe it is best to highlight one's intentions in the beginning to ensure there are no misunderstandings. Then, some believe you should let it happen whenever time permits. Either way, it must be mentioned because marriage is most often the target.

If you were to take a poll, you would see that virtually no one mentioned marriage on their first date. It is a touchy topic, but the sooner it is discussed, the better. Why? Because you do not want to be on date number 20 and find out the other person has no intention of getting married while that is your goal. Essentially, you must determine what is best for you regarding when to bring up the topic of marriage. However, you must also keep in mind that the longer you wait, you just might be wasting valuable time that you cannot get back.

It is imperative that marriage be discussed early on because you do not know which phase of life the other person is in unless you speak up. Depending upon the phase, the person might appear ready but may not be in the phase best suited for you at that moment.

Let's explore three phases of life that may help you when trying to pinpoint where your potential mate is in their thought process.

1. **Beer Phase:** This is the flat phase. Those in this phase of life have not figured out exactly what they want to do in life. They are canned into normality that keeps them mentally bottled up. They have more words than actions but still seem as if they could be the one for a stable

person. They paint great pictures, but you must not get hung up with them. They have energy until they must commit long-term. They keep making the same mistakes and seemingly do not want to get out of their own way. They are headstrong in doing things their way and will cause you many headaches if you choose to stay with them. They are also more selfish than they realize and are not ready for a long-term commitment. They have unpredictable schedules. Many of them are looking for someone to take care of them and are master manipulators who have no remorse concerning hurting someone's heart. Some have out-of-this-world potential to become stable, but distractions and stubbornness keep them from progressing to the stable phase. Being a responsible person is not a strong suit for some of them. In many instances, they are a combination of the prior three sentences. They become flat faster than anyone else in other phases of life. Be careful because those in this phase are most likely juggling multiple relationships like they breathe oxygen.

2. **Liquor Phase:** This is the turbulence phase. The people in this phase have a mixture of distractions that prevent them from gaining stability in their lives. They are almost ready for a stable person but need more time. They have particular issues that prevent them from having true stability. Until they get their affairs and priorities in order, they will not be suitable for a stable person. In particular instances, a stable person can help them transition to the stable phase of life, but that translates to the stable person being willing to endure the ensuing headaches that will follow. Be careful because these people might not be ready to commit and cause a stable person to fall into the turbulence phase.

They hesitate to make critical sacrifices for the relationship and believe their excuses are justifiable. They could eventually become draining because of their dependency upon the stable person. They are more trustworthy than those in the beer phase. They are almost ready for a long-term commitment. If they do not transition to the stable phase of life soon, they will become flat, too.

3. **Wine Phase:** This is the stable phase. Those in this phase are progressing well in life with minimum or zero distractions. They most likely have multiple streams of income and are laser-focused on accomplishing tasks. They are willing to make sacrifices for their relationship without hesitation. They are more trustworthy and patient than those in the beer and liquor phases. Although they have stability in life, they are still receptive to things that help them, and others get better. They tend to fall for those in the turbulence phase because they see great potential, but they must be mindful because that potential could also be a trap. They are locked into peace, truth, and progress. They continue to get better with time and are ready for a long-term commitment.

The overall objective is to "Be in peace, not pieces!" You must do your due diligence before you commit to a relationship. It does not matter how good that book cover looks because you are still responsible for examining the contents prior to making an investment.

She's Ready at 18... He's Ready at 38!

Due Diligence Assistance

There are many reasons why people get married. It is my hope that the number one reason is because of love. Unfortunately, love is not always the reason. Some people get married because they have children together. Some marry out of cultural traditions. Some do so because their church pressures them. Others might not want to be single any longer and countless other reasons. However, when they get married, they must deal with their decision.

One of the most important things both parties must clarify from the start is their expectations of the other person. Highlighting expectations before marriage is a must because it is like painting a picture before placing it in a frame. Unfortunately, some people frame pictures before trying to paint them. After highlighting expectations, please consider the following before getting married:

- **Don't allow a test drive or test drives:** Many people say you must live with someone before getting married. That is not so, which is why you go on multiple dates and ask countless questions about one another and expect great detail to each inquiry.
- **Don't look for someone to carry you:** Some people look for others to take care of them, but both parties should desire to take care of one another. Some people have been raised with the mentality that the woman doesn't have to work, while others have been raised with the mindset that both parties must contribute their equal share. Essentially, the key to a good relationship is when both parties contribute to the relationship in many ways. It is not a good idea to depend on one income in this era,

but it is still happening. Please communicate openly about this topic before getting married.

- **Don't lower your standards:** You should have high standards because you should think highly of yourself. If you lower your standards, you could raise your average of strikeouts! Keep your standards high until you hit a home run.
- **Don't compromise being compatible:** It is said the opposites attract—and they do, but they can also subtract. There must be common ground. Compatibility leads to better communication and more joyful activities together. A commonality of thoughts stimulates the relationship. Without compatibility, the relationship could go stale quickly.
- **Don't try to park a truck in a doghouse:** This is when a good person tries to force a relationship with a known cheater. That often happens when the good person allows sex or money to influence the relationship. Please do not attempt to do that, no matter how attractive the person is or how good they make you feel. Just like you shouldn't try to park a truck in a doghouse, a good person shouldn't try to park their peace of mind in a polluted place. They just might run the risk of getting infected.
- **Don't select your mate based on the world's standards:** The media and other worldly programming venues have planted misleading seeds that have significantly impacted how people select their mates. Look deeply into how inaccurate their seeds are because the world paints many fairytales that turn into nightmares. Please change the channel or unplug from the world's teachings.

- **Don't neglect to check your mate's financial situation:** Don't set yourself up for failure! Not checking your potential mate's financial status is a recipe for disaster. Please review one another's credit reports and write down your collective obligations. A mate who refuses to do this most likely has something detrimental to hide. Please do not waver in at least discussing your financial statuses.
- **Don't overlook how they interact with family members:** Some people paint their best portraits when they are among family and friends. Initially, they can hide themselves well, but their interactions with others will paint other portraits after a period of time to help you see who they truly are. In some cases, the family members and friends will tell you things your mate does not want you to know. Pay attention!
- **Don't neglect to discuss romance and sex:** These are two of the most essential pillars of a relationship but are often the least talked about before and during the marriage. Romance and sexual diets must be discussed in the beginning to avoid misunderstandings. Keep in mind that not everyone has the same experiences in romance and sex, making them glaring priorities. Please make them a priority. Additionally, some people's passion is like that of a candle burning, while others are like a forest fire. The forest fire-like passion can consume the candle, but the flame will die out if the candle-burning passion resists. The candle will find that it is nearly impossible to reduce the passion of the forest, but sometimes, it works through great sacrifice. Communicate and invest in one another's passion because a lack of passion can become a flame retardant in your marriage.

- **Don't dismiss marriage counseling/mentorship:** Some individuals have marital nuggets that can help you avoid pitfalls. Consider mentors who have been married for over 20 years. You can never have too much wisdom! Please don't choose the "trial by error method" nor allow experience to be your only teacher.

She's Ready at 18... He's Ready at 38!

Hurdles or Walls

Essentially, we must live with our decisions to be married if we are married to the right mate. Sometimes, we do not find out everything about our mate until after marriage. Rushed unions can cause us to dig holes that are extremely challenging to climb out of. Some of the things we found out after marriage may make us want to file for divorce because they are things that remain a wedge in our relationships.

However, there are some things you can work through that requires a collective effort but sometimes remain absent. Many individuals are oblivious to the topics because of various reasons, but they must be highlighted to help them make better decisions. Following are some examples that have manifested after marriage:

- ➢ **Choosing to lick honey from thorns:** Many individuals project to outsiders that all is well within their marriage, but truthfully, the marriage is toxic. Pride, money, traditions, children, and other factors help keep them together, but they know the marriage is not what it's supposed to be. They continue to project a lie while they continue to become toxic. The only way to remove toxicity from marriage is not to be the toxic one or ones within it. Remember this: When material or flesh remains in toxic waste for prolonged periods, they could be damaged beyond repair. Similarly, that is what you must stay out of or get out of toxic marriages. The truth shall set you free and is as sweet as honey.
- ➢ **Daddy's baby girl:** A woman who her daddy has spoiled is normally not a deal-breaker, but there are some instances when the woman expects her husband to

be just like her dad. That most often impacts rushed marriages that prevent the husband from seeing the signs prior to the marriage. While it is great that her father spoiled his baby girl, she must not expect her husband to be able to imitate her dad's output. In some instances, her father has fostered an environment that conditioned her thinking. It handicaps her ability to be independent because he never allowed her to endure things that could have helped mold her to be strong and independent. Then, there are other instances where being daddy's baby girl helped the woman because she saw her dad display how a man takes care of his responsibilities. It only becomes an issue when the wife starts to verbally assault her husband for not being exactly like her father or if she has internally developed a snowball of dislike for her husband for not spoiling her just like her dad did. That is why both parties must discuss their expectations of one another prior to marriage.

➢ **Momma's boy:** A momma's boy is normally not a deal-breaker, either, but there are a few situations when he has been spoiled by his mom, to the point where he expects his woman to be like his mom. The momma's boy most likely developed an umbilical cord-like dependency with his mom that he would expect to have with his woman. That type of connection can negatively impact a relationship, especially if the man has not fully matured into an independent person. His mindset would be centered on the umbilical cord dependency to help him prosper in life, and if the woman cannot foster that same type of dependency, then the man would internally develop a snowball of dislike for his wife for not fostering a similar dependency connection like his mom did. That is also why it is imperative for both parties to discuss the expectations they have for one another before marriage.

- **Controlling person:** If you frequently interact with your mate before marriage, you could see a sprinkle of controlling tactics. Younger people actually rely on location services and aggressively monitor/control their mates' social media actions. Older individuals aggressively control their mates' relationships with their family members and coworkers. A controlling person will most likely do their best to isolate their mate, too. It is very important that you try to identify that type of person early because their ways can influence them to be abusive, too. Please do not take a controlling person lightly. Know that you are not the remedy for them. Please highlight to them their controlling ways and, if they remain in denial, pray for them or seek counseling if you still desire to be with such a person.
- **Naggers:** This is applicable to both males and females. Sometimes, there is justified nagging such as when the other person repeats things that irritate their mate, which triggers a "nagging response." In other instances, the nagger is a habitual complainer. That type of nagger pushes the other person away, causing the mate not to want to be in their presence. This can be overcome with proper communication, though, but not in all persons.
- **Liars:** They are who they are before marriage. If you listen to family members and friends, they will exploit the liars for you. If you interact more frequently with your mate prior to marriage, you could see sprinkles of lies. Please highlight to them their lying ways. Hopefully, they will change. Liars can become controlling and delusional, which can cause you to

waste more than your precious time. Please pray for them or seek counseling for them while protecting yourself if you desire to be with such a person.

- **Cheaters:** Most of the time, you won't see the signs of a cheater. If you do see them before marriage, then you definitely should not marry that person. That is also why you shouldn't try to smother them in the beginning or during the marriage to try and stop them from cheating. A cheater is going to cheat before and during the marriage if they can. Unfortunately, you can't cure a cheater. Please know they can also become controlling and delusional, which will cause you to waste more than your valuable time. Remember this: "They who tame their appetite will focus on one meal and also avoid more than food poison!" Please pray for them or seek counseling for them while protecting yourself if you desire to be with such a person.
- **Abusers:** Most often, you will not see the signs of an abuser. If you do see them acting wrongly before marriage, you definitely should not marry them. The types of abuse are physical, sexual, emotional, mental, and neglect. No one should experience any, let alone all of them. Unfortunately, they are just like liars and cheaters in that you cannot cure them. Please know they can also become controlling and delusional, which may cause you to waste more than your precious time. Please pray for them or seek counseling for them while protecting yourself if you desire to be with such a person.

Lastly, **"Don't lose yourself!"** We can endure many things, but abusers, cheaters, liars, and controlling people should be removed from the consideration list. The examples listed above are intended to emphasize that you truly have to study your mate before marriage. Essentially, don't become a patient while being patient! In other words, get out of a bad relationship before it ruins you.

Skin Deep

A handsome man could also mean he is a handful, just like him being fine could also be a complete waste of your time!

A beautiful, sexy woman does not exclude her from being messy, just like her being pretty does not exclude her from being petty.

In essence, sometimes one's outer appearance can be overrated and could get you caught up in a mental or physical bind. Look deeper than the flesh, as doing so will help you do a better job at protecting your heart, soul, and mind!

Mates

In the beginning, you might start as soulmates. Then the issues of life cause you to act like primates, making you become cellmates. But God wants you to get back to being more than housemates and definitely more than bedmates. So, get back in the love boat and become greater shipmates while transitioning from inmates to win-mates!

Biblical Principles of Marriage

The biblical perspective of marriage starts at the beginning of the Holy Bible in the Book of Genesis:

"So God created man in his own image, in the image of God he created him; male and female he created them. And God blessed them. And God said to them, 'Be fruitful and multiply and fill the earth and subdue it and have dominion over the fish of the sea and over the birds of the heavens and over every living thing that moves on the earth.'" (Genesis 1:27-28)

Take a moment to read that passage again and focus on the commandment. Notice how, together, the male and female have dominion. God did not speak to them individually; He addressed them as a couple. That highlights the power within their unity and agreement, as well as that they are a true power couple because God put them together.

Another key passage comes from the Book of Ecclesiastes:

"Two are better than one because they have a good reward for their toil. For if they fall, one will lift up his fellow. But woe to him who is alone when he falls and has not another to lift him up!" (Ecclesiastes 4:9-10)

The Husband

Genesis 2:18-25

"And the LORD God said, 'It is not good that the man should be alone; I will make him a help meet for him."

(Notice the Word says "help meet." That highlights that the man needs help, and since the Word does not specify exactly where the man needs help, we must agree that there are multiple areas where his help meet can assist. She can help him meet goals and accomplishments that he cannot do by himself. She is purposed by God and of great importance in that God did not specify a limit on how she helps him. That is because she brings the favor that he does not have, and it is that favor that will help him meet his purpose and more. Also, the man must not lose sight of his help meet assisting him in both the earth and spirit realms.)

"And out of the ground, the LORD God formed every beast of the field, and every fowl of the air; and brought them unto Adam to see what he would call them: and whatsoever Adam called every living creature, that was the name thereof. And Adam gave names to all cattle, and to the fowl of the air, and to every beast of the field..."

(What does the naming of those things have to do with finding someone comparable to Adam? Adam also had to know what was not comparable to him. Those creatures (cattle, birds, and beasts) also helped him spiritually develop into the husband he needed to be. As it was written, the word 'cattle' was associated with cows, bulls, oxen, goats, sheep, calves, and other livestock. Cattle symbolize substance, truth, acquisition, and sacrifice. The husband must provide all of those things for his family. The spiritual revelation of cattle represents the coming Messiah, who is the Truth and Bread of Life who paid the ransom for us through becoming the sacrificial Lamb of God. The fowl of the air are birds. Birds symbolize freedom, wisdom, and elevation. The husband should ensure his family's freedom through the manifold wisdom of God, which allows his family to prosper. The spiritual revelation in the text is the representation of the Holy Spirit and His works for the body of Christ. The beasts are wild animals that roam the fields. Most of them are not friendly to humans. The husband must be prepared to win against all types of beasts. The spiritual revelation in the text symbolizes spiritual wickedness. The husband must keep on the Armor of God and maximize the weapons of his warfare to defeat all spiritual enemies.)

"...but for Adam, there was not found a help meet for him."

(Who was looking? God said, "I will make him a helper comparable to him." Man will look for himself and make mistake after mistake, but through God, the man will receive a daughter of God who will be his overflow. Through the usage of his natural eyes rather than his spiritual eye, the spiritual revelation is that man will choose wrong and miss blessings, which is why he must rely on God to help him select his mate. After all, God knows the plans He has for every man.)

"And the LORD God caused a deep sleep to fall upon Adam, and he slept: and He took one of his ribs, and closed up the flesh instead thereof; and the rib, which the LORD God had taken from man, made he a woman, and brought her unto the man. And Adam said, 'This is now bone of my bones, and flesh of my flesh: she shall be called Woman, because she was taken out of Man.'"

That was a supernatural sign and wonder that only the Creator could do, which was also needed to continue the manifestation of humanity. The Lord God had first made man in His image, so fittingly, the woman was made from God's first image. At that time, Adam was clean; thus, the woman was clean as well. The spiritual revelation is that the Bride (Body of Christ) came out of Christ and, upon His return, the whole body in the earthly realm will not be joined with the Groom but rather the rib (remnant) will be pulled (caught up) to be with Him forever.

"Therefore, shall a man leave his father and his mother, and shall cleave unto his wife: and they shall be one flesh."

(The man must separate so that he and his wife can stay together! That is more spiritual than physical. Parents have spiritual assignments with good and evil (via the Enemy) assigned to them, which could tamper with the oneness with his wife. He cannot depend on them anymore but must depend on the Lord God to be his Provider, Sustainer, Strong Tower, and Teacher as he leads his marriage. The spiritual revelation is that at the point of the Son's sacrifice, He had to leave the presence of His Father and eventually, Mother Earth, to become the Groom for His Bride.)

"And they were both naked, the man and his wife, and were not ashamed."

(They started their journey with clean hands and pure hearts. They must maintain them in oneness by repenting together while forgiving and asking for forgiveness together. The spiritual revelation is that after the Groom and Bride are united, they shall remain spiritually clean forevermore.)

****

A woman of God should prefer a man who has accepted Christ Jesus as his Lord and Savior and who walks upright in obedience to God, led by the Holy Spirit, while also aspiring to be the man mentioned in Psalm 1:1-3 before and during the marriage:

"Blessed is the man that walketh not in the counsel of the ungodly, nor standeth in the way of sinners, nor sitteth in the seat of the scornful. But his delight is in the law of the LORD; and in His law doth he meditate day and night. And he shall be like a tree planted by the rivers of water, that bringeth forth his fruit in his season; his leaf also shall not wither; and whatsoever he doeth shall prosper."

In some instances, the man hasn't completely developed into the man he needs to be, but at a minimum, he should be a Christian in obedience to God if he is going to be a husband to a God-given bride. Although a man was not created for a woman's sake ("...for indeed, man was not created for the woman's sake, but woman for the man's sake..." 1 Corinthians 11:9), he must strive to be in a position to receive the woman God provides for him. If he pleases God, he will not have to stress about finding his bride, as God will ensure he finds her.

As God provides her, the man will find his bride to be priceless ("Who can find a virtuous woman? For her price is far above rubies..." Proverbs 31:10). A virtuous woman is most compatible with the man mentioned in Psalm 1:1-3. She will also come with checked baggage for her flight into marriage. Favor is the supernatural content within her checked baggage to help her husband.

The Wife

It is said that behind every great man is a great woman, but I must ask: Who is behind a great woman? GOD IS! He empowers her to make an impact, not just an impression, which He highlights in His Word:

> *"He who finds a wife finds a good thing and obtains favor from the Lord"* (Proverbs 18:22).

(She is a good thing because she believes in Christ as a daughter of God, and favor accompanies her. Why, then, does the man receive favor? Because the wife God gives is also one of His daughters whom man cannot take care of alone. God ensures His daughters have more than man to provide for them. The favor is also seen as a supernatural gift to the man specifically assigned to help the union prosper. Additionally, the Word does not say "a favor" or place a limit on the promise, which could translate to meaning perpetual favor.)

Notice a lot of time was not spent on the wife. Why? Well, there is no debate that women mature faster than men — an intentional design by God — which makes them ready to join in matrimony and leveled for the purposes assigned to their union. The Word shows us that the woman was born ready (refer back to Genesis 1:21-25). Although many women have been negatively affected by past relationships, they will still be ready for whomever God created just for them. That is also why women of today must rely on the Holy Spirit to help them in discerning the husband God has for them. Sadly, countless men manipulate women, but the Holy Spirit will help women identify lies, witchcraft, and truth. Although the Holy Spirit is readily available, the woman has a responsibility, too. She must also do her part in discerning if the man is a good man of God.

After knowing the man is, indeed, a Christian, obedient to God, led by the Holy Spirit, and walking as the Psalms 1:1-3 man, she can also use the following verses to help her receive the good man God has for her. (Be mindful that a woman might meet the man who is to be her husband before he has fully matured into the complete man of God for her. Therefore, the Holy Spirit's help is critical!)

> ➢ **Psalm 37:23** – *"The steps of a good man are ordered by the LORD: and he delighteth in his way."* (His steps include blessings for his household.)
> ➢ **Proverbs 12:2** – *"A good man obtaineth favour of the LORD: but a man of wicked devices will He condemn."* (Being a good man who obtains favor and has a good wife who brings favor is called overflow and comes with possible perpetual favor.)
> ➢ **Proverbs 13:22** – *"A good man leaveth an inheritance to his children's children: and the wealth of the sinner is laid up for the just."* (Already knowing he will leave an inheritance to his children's children is a blessing.)
> ➢ **James 5:16** – *"Confess your faults one to another, and pray one for another, that ye may be healed. The effectual fervent prayer of a righteous man availeth much."* (The effectual fervent prayer of a righteous man is also a plus for a marriage.)

One thing is for certain: A woman of God will submit to a man of God before ever submitting to a man of the world. That is also why the woman should use Psalm 1:1-3 as a guide to help her discern who her husband should be. She must focus on being a good thing of the Lord, and He will ensure she is connected to the one who walks uprightly via the Holy Spirit, similarly to what is mentioned in Psalm 84:11:

"For the LORD God is a sun and shield: the LORD will give grace and glory: no good thing will He withhold from them that walk uprightly."

The woman was the first one made in the earthly realm to help another soul. She is anointed to be a magnet of addition, not subtraction. She completes the equation of progress and helps to magnify a relationship. She is not just another link in the chain. She helps to strengthen the links within the chain. She walks with her husband, not behind him.

The Union

When you think of marriage, you should think of love, unity, power, and agreement. The Word teaches us that agreement is powerful:

"Again, I say unto you, that if two of you shall agree on earth as touching anything that they shall ask, it shall be done for them of My Father, which is in Heaven" (Matthew 18:19).

Agreements between God's children are powerful—and the Enemy hates it! Agreements between God's children create an unbreakable force that gains momentum fueled by faith. The agreements have supernatural power in the spirit and earth realms, which is why they must be treated as sacred arrangements.

Marriage is not a job, but it is always a work in progress. That progress is supposed to be positive and made in love. The husband is to uplift his wife in a manner that she has no doubt she is the most valuable queen alive. She should know in her heart that her husband would sacrifice his life for her every day if he could. She should feel protected and without worries. All of those attributes are great, but Ephesians 5:25 – 33 explains it best as to how the husband should treat his wife:

"Husbands, love your wives, as Christ loved the church and gave Himself up for her, that He might sanctify her, having cleansed her by the washing of water with the Word, so that He might present the church to Himself in splendor, without spot or wrinkle or any such thing, that she might be holy and without blemish. In the same way, husbands should love their wives as their own bodies. He who loves his wife loves himself. For no one ever hated his own flesh, but nourishes and cherishes it, just as Christ does the church..."

Additionally, the husband should also use 1 Peter 3:7 to help guide him in being the husband God intended him to be to His daughter:

"Likewise, husbands, live with your wives in an understanding way, showing honor to the woman as the weaker vessel, since they are heirs with you of the grace of life, so that your prayers may not be hindered."

As the man prepares and becomes that man of God, the woman then receives him as such. But, if he has strayed into the world, then she would be less likely to honor him as expected. A woman of God desires to see Christ in her man, which is why she is tuned into 1 Corinthians 11:3:

"But I would have you know that the head of every man in Christ and the head of the woman is the man; and the head of Christ is God."

She abides in the Lord who is within the man, rather than abiding in the man himself. A woman of God will not compromise her abiding under any circumstance. She is captured in the Spirit of the Lord more than the things that enamor the flesh, unlike non-women of God who are captured in the fleshly attractions of man. As she looks forward to her blessed union, she has no issues adhering to Ephesians 5:22-24:

"Wives, submit yourselves unto your own husbands, as unto the LORD. For the Husband is the head of the church: and He is the Saviour of the body. Therefore, as the church is subject unto Christ, so let the wives be to their own husbands in everything."

Surely, the man of God knows he has a priceless gift from God who helps him physically, spiritually, and mentally, which is why she is also his crown, as seen in Proverbs 12:4:

"An excellent wife is the crown of her husband, but she who causes shame is like rottenness in his bones."

She does more than complement, as he trusts similarly to what we see in Proverbs 31:11:

"The heart of her husband safely trusts her, so he will have no lack of gain. She does him good and not evil all the days of her life."

She is his overflow, and he is her surplus. Their spiritual compatibilities allow them to flow in almost everything they do. Being able to flow together is a wondrous feeling within a relationship and helps to stabilize the union.

Remember this: Both the husband and wife have responsibilities to protect their marriage, knowing that God's hands are in it. They must keep strengthening one another and ensuring the fire stays lit within the marriage. They must be receptive to improving all areas of the marriage with no wavering. A marriage must transform from being a work in progress to progressing from the work put in it. The marriage must be protected from all enemies, foreign and domestic, including family members, friends, and anyone in the ear of both parties, all while keeping in mind Mark 10:9:

"Therefore, what God has joined together, let no one separate."

Lastly, a marriage God has put together will prosper! It will be strong! It will be protected and not neglected! It will produce good fruit! It will be an example for others to follow! It will not crack under pressure! It will be empowered by Christ Jesus and led by the Holy Spirit. Shalom.

She's Ready at 18… He's Ready at 38!

Your Lawn (Relationship)

A great gardener will ensure the lawn's and garden's soil are good, have the proper seeds, know when to apply the proper fertilizer, keep the lawn properly watered, prosper no matter the season, and ensure the lawn gets the proper amount of sunlight.

A great lawn can increase the value of an establishment. Choosing the proper seed is essential when growing a great lawn. There should be zero compromises in selecting the proper seed because if the seeds are incompatible, they will not grow properly, thus withering after only a few seasons. One of the most important parts of the lawn is the soil. The soil stays strong because of water, fertilizer, mowing, and the sun. Please take care of your lawn!

Lawn = Relationship
Establishment = True Love
Seed = Significant Other
Seasons = Trials and Tribulations
Soil = Foundation of the Relationship is Belief in the Almighty God
Water = Allowing the Holy Spirit to Guide the Relationship
Fertilizer = Praying Together, Spending Time with the Lord Together, and Studying the Word Together
Sun = Christ Jesus

About the Author

Calvin Brown is an Apostle of Jesus Christ with the indwelling of the Holy Spirit. God has blessed him to lead the Remnant of Christ's Kingdom International Apostolic Ministry (ROCK I AM) and the 365 Days of Praying and Fasting ministry. His wife, Prophet Kenya Brown, assists with leading those ministries.

God uses him to support various ministry efforts worldwide to include the Mercies of Hope International Ministries in Kampala, Uganda. As led by the Holy Spirit, he will continue partnering with other ministries to spread the Gospel of Jesus Christ internationally, help fellow Christians, and help communities.

His first book was published in 2012 and is titled "A Gift from the Holy Spirit: Should We All Speak In Tongues?" His second book was published in 2020, and it is titled "365 Days In The Word." The Holy Spirit is also guiding him to lead other projects in the future that will assist the Body of Christ.

Calvin thrives to please God and will continue his relentless efforts in spreading the Gospel of Jesus Christ around the earth.

Calvin Brown